Keys

26
Weekly
Devotionals

Phil Stern

© Copyright 2012 Phil Stern. All rights reserved.

Unless otherwise noted, all scripture is from the New King James Version, Copyright © 1982, Thomas Nelson, Inc. All rights reserved.

Scripture designated (ESV) is from the English Standard Version. Copyright © 2001 by Crossway Bibles, a division of Good News Publishers.

Scripture designated (KJV) is from the King James Version.

Scripture designated (NASB) is from the New American Standard Bible (1995 Update). Copyright © 1981, 1998 THE LOCKMAN FOUNDATION, A Corporation Not for Profit, La Habra, California. All Rights Reserved. International Copyright Secured.

Scripture designated (NASB77) is from the New American Standard Bible (1977 Edition) Copyright © The Lockman Foundation 1960, 1962, 1963, 1968, 1971, 1972, 1973, 1975, 1977, 1988. All Rights Reserved. International Copyright Secured.

Scripture designated (NIV) is from the New International Version. Copyright © 1973, 1978, 1984, International Bible Society. All rights reserved.

Scripture designated (NLT) is from *Holy Bible,* New Living Translation, copyright © 1996, 2004 by Tyndale Charitable Trust. All rights reserved.

Table of Contents

Keys to Joy
      3 Keys to Finding Joy in Life's Struggles. 1

Keys to Overcoming Part I
      Overcoming Life's Disappointments & Difficulties Part I. 9

Keys to Overcoming Part II
      Overcoming Life's Disappointments & Difficulties Part II. 13

Keys to Determination
      Making the Determined Effort!. 19

Keys to Flavor Your World
      Being a Christian in a Non-Christian World. 25

Keys to Values
      The Importance of VALUES. 29

Keys to Changing Values
      How To Contend With Changing Values. 33

Keys to Overcoming Fear
      500 Fears — You Can Overcome Them!. 39

Keys to Keeping a Marriage
      What Really Keeps a Marriage Together?. 47

Keys to Remembering
      10 Ways to Stop Forgetting Things & Keep Your Word! 51

Keys to New Beginnings
      Giving the New Year a Kick Start. 55

Keys to Change Your Year
    4 Ways To Kick Start Your New Year. 59

Keys to Life
    10 Reasons NOT to Read Your Bible This Year. 63

Keys to the Marketplace Part I
    Differences in the Roles of Kings and Priests Part I. . 67

Keys to the Marketplace Part II
    Differences in the Roles of Kings and Priests Part II.. 71

Keys to the Marketplace Part III
    Kings, Priests, and Prophets…Working Together. . . . 75

Keys to the Marketplace Part IV
    The Business Leader's (Kings) Prayer Life
        Asking W h a t s o e v e r !.. 81

Keys to the Marketplace Part V
    Breaking the Lies of a Poverty Mentality. 87

Keys to the Marketplace Part VI
    The Kingdom's Effect in Our Lives Part I.. 91

Keys to the Marketplace Part VII
    The Kingdom's Effect in Our Lives Part II. 97

Keys to the Marketplace Part VIII
    The 1 Essential Habit of Every Effective Leader. . . . 103

Keys to the Marketplace Part IX
    Skills Vs Gifts. 107

Keys to the Land Part I
    12 Keys to Understanding the Land of Israel
        Part I. 109

Keys to the Land Part II
    12 Keys to Understanding the Land of Israel
        Part II............................. 115

Keys To The Land Part III
    12 Keys to Understanding the Land of Israel
        Part III............................ 119

Keys to the Land Part IV
    12 Keys to Understanding the Land of Israel
        Part IV............................ 127

ABOUT THIS DEVOTIONAL...

This devotional is a compilation of weekly devotionals I have been writing for several years and sending out to several thousand email addresses every Monday morning. The devotions are short and hopefully will provoke you to think more deeply on the each individual subject. My prayer is that you will be blessed and ministered to through each one or through the ones that God leads you to.

The first devotion book I published titled "***The Focused Life***" was released with topics dealing with focus. This devotional has a main stream yet with various topics. The stream is "Keys" and the topics are "The Market Place," "The Land of Israel" and many stand alone keys such as "Keys To Joy," "Keys to Overcoming," "Keys to Determination," etc.

ACKNOWLEDGMENTS...

I want to thank my dear friend Mike Hodge, who labored above and beyond the call of duty to edit this book for me. Mike does excellent work and would love to do your project as well. Thanks Mike! Joel Funkhouser is another person who has also helped me get these projects across the finish line. Joel does all the art work and cover design. He too would be ready to help you if you ever need an excellent cover design or website. He is the best!!

I thank Gaines Dittrich for opening my eyes to the "Market Place" and how Kings and Priests are to be connected for the furtherance of the Kingdom of God. Gaines, thank you for being the king that you are and the example we need today. I thank Rabbi Curt Landry for connecting me with the Land of Israel. I will never be the same again after the experience I had while in Israel. I credit Gaines and Sandy Dittrich for being obedient to pursue my wife and me to make that journey two years ago.

For weekly devotionals...

If you would like to receive "**the devotional**" from me weekly, go to the Link Ministry website at www.linkmin.org, and in the top right of the home page there is a place to register your email address. A weekly devotion will be sent to you every Monday morning.

devo 1

Keys to Joy

3 Keys to Finding Joy in Life's Struggles

How can we completely break free from our past so that we can live successful and productive lives in the here and now? It is possible and you can begin the process if you apply the instructions from the Bible.

> My brethren, count it all joy when you fall into various trials, knowing that the testing of your faith produces patience. But let patience have its **perfect work, that you may be perfect and complete, lacking nothing**.
> James 1:2-4 Emphasis added

How many of us really take this verse seriously? We laugh and say, "Yea, oh sure, uh huh!" But the truth is, we can completely break free from our past and live successful and productive lives

Keys to Joy
3 Keys to Finding Joy in Life's Struggles

in the here and now. There are a number of things which cause hardship in our lives. Things such as sicknesses, family tragedies, out of work, financial difficulties, family problems, job stress, business failures, changes in our lives, major calamities such as earthquakes, tornados, floods, etc. These things are a given, but Jesus says, "be of good cheer." He is saying that we must learn how to find joy in the midst of life's hardships, because He has given us the truth to overcome everything!

> "These things I have spoken to you, that in Me you may have peace. In the world you will have tribulation; but be of good cheer, I have overcome the world."
> John 16:33

Three reasons why storms come into our life:
- They help keep us on track with important things in our lives.
- They make us look for answers from God because we have exhausted our strength.
- Struggles and hardships sift out the impurities in our lives.

HOW THEN DO WE FIND JOY IN THE TRIAL OF HARDSHIP?

> "Behold, God is my salvation, I will trust and not be afraid; 'For YAH, the LORD, is my strength and my song; He also has become my salvation.' Therefore with joy you will draw water from the wells of salvation."
> Isaiah 12:2-3

Keys to Joy
3 Keys to Finding Joy in Life's Struggles

1. We Must Completely Let Go of The Past

> Brethren, I do not count myself to have apprehended; but one thing I do, **forgetting those things which are behind** and reaching forward to those things which are ahead...
> Philippians 3:13 (NASB77) Emphasis added

Until we are really free from the past, we will never have the joy that is needed to deal with today's problems and trials. There is so much for us to reach forward to with a sense of anticipation and hope, but we must let go of the past before the joy and hope of the future can really settle in.

2. We must Have a Vision That Is Greater than the Struggle

> Where there is no revelation, the people cast off restraint; but happy is he who keeps the law.
> Proverbs 29:18

It is vision that sustains us in the midst of life's hardships, because it gives us the ability to see beyond that which is taking place in our lives momentarily. It enables us to not lose heart in the midst of the problem. As we continue to focus on the vision God has given us of what He has in store for us, as well as the blessing of eternal bliss, we are able to see that whatever we are going through is only a momentary affliction.

> Therefore we do not lose heart. Even though our outward man is perishing, yet the inward man is being renewed day by day. For our light affliction, which is but for a moment, is working for us a far more exceeding and eternal weight of glory, while we do not look at the things which are seen, but at

Keys to Joy
3 Keys to Finding Joy in Life's Struggles

> the things which are not seen. For the things which are seen are temporary, but the things which are not seen are eternal.
> 2 Corinthians. 4:16-18

In one of Germany's famous art galleries, a painting called "Cloud Lane" hangs at the end of a long dark hall. It appears at first to be a huge, ugly mass of confused color, unattractive and foreboding. Upon closer examination, however, you see an innumerable company of angels. Theodore Cuyler writes, "How often the soul that is frightened by a trial sees nothing but a conglomeration of broken expectations. But if he analyzes the situation from a position of faith, he will soon discover that the cloud is God's wonderful chariot of providence, full of angels of mercy."

In Genesis 37:5-11 there is the great example of Joseph who experienced his share of hardships. His brothers hated him because of his dreams, they sold him into slavery, he was put into prison for something he didn't do and yet in all of this he was able to find joy. The reason was because he had a vision that was greater than any of the struggles he was going through.

> And the keeper of the prison committed to Joseph's hand all the prisoners who were in the prison; whatever they did there, it was his doing.
> Genesis 39:22

Because of his positive attitude of joy in the midst of difficulty, Joseph saw his dreams come to fulfillment. Joseph had some choices he had to make. He could have taken on a victim mentality by feeling sorry for himself. He could have gotten bitter toward those who had done him wrong or he could find joy in the difficulty because of the vision that was yet before him.

Keys to Joy
3 Keys to Finding Joy in Life's Struggles

> But as for you, you meant evil against me; but God meant it for good, in order to bring it about as it is this day, to save many people alive.
> Genesis 50:20

3. We must Focus on the Growth this Trial Will Bring in Our Lives.

God has always desired to use the hardships in our lives to teach us to rely on Him and to use them as an opportunity for growth and maturity. Our growth and maturity comes out of the hard lessons of life, not the easy ones.

> And not only that, but we also glory in tribulations, knowing that tribulation produces perseverance; and perseverance, character; and character, hope. Now hope does not disappoint, because the love of God has been poured out in our hearts by the Holy Spirit who was given to us.
> Romans 5:3-5

I was driving down a bumpy country road when I saw a bag of cement beside the road. It appeared to have fallen off a delivery truck as it hit one of the bumps in the rough road. Being a person who does not like to see anything wasted, I stopped to pick up the lost bag of cement. When I reached down to pick up this heavy bag, to my surprise I discovered it was not soft and limber, as I had expected, but it had solidified into an immovable piece of cement.

God spoke to me through this; Often our lives are like that bag of cement. They take on shapes that were not intended and become hardened in that shape. That bag of cement was meant to become part of some beautiful structure, but because it did not reach its place of service, it became a useless rock that looked like a bag of cement. God wants to make your life into something

Keys to Joy
3 Keys to Finding Joy in Life's Struggles

beautiful. Don't let His purpose be thwarted by a bump in the road of life.

Often, when trouble comes, our natural tendency is to focus on self and the problem and to turn inward, which only leads to losing our joy. As a result we develop a survival mentality rather than an overcoming mentality. The overcoming mentality is what leads to spiritual growth and maturity in the Lord as well as success in our lives.

4. Finally... We must Learn to Trust in the Lord in All Things

> But let all those rejoice who put their trust in You; Let them ever shout for joy, because You defend them; Let those also who love Your name Be joyful in You. For You, O LORD, will bless the righteous; with favor You will surround him as with a shield.
> Psalms 5:11-12

Our ability to continually trust in God is a very strong key element in our ability to find joy in the midst of life's hardships, because trust enables us to know deep within our heart and soul that everything is really going to be ok. It enables us to not get anxious.

Meditate on these scriptures this week:

> Trust in the LORD, and do good; Dwell in the land, and feed on His faithfulness. Delight yourself also in the LORD, And He shall give you the desires of your heart. Psalms 37:3-4

Keys to Joy
3 Keys to Finding Joy in Life's Struggles

Rejoice in the Lord always. Again I will say, rejoice! Let your gentleness be known to all men. The Lord is at hand. Be anxious for nothing, but in everything by prayer and supplication, with thanksgiving, let your requests be made known to God; and the peace of God, which surpasses all understanding, will guard your hearts and minds through Christ Jesus.
Philippians 4:4-7

Those who trust in the LORD Are like Mount Zion, Which cannot be moved, but abides forever.
Psalms 125:1

devo 2

Keys to Overcoming
Part I

Overcoming Life's Disappointments & Difficulties
Part I

I want to share with you about having the kind of faith that is able to overcome life's disappointments and difficulties. When we learn how to face all of life's situations correctly and with God's direction, we can have a hope that will get us through anything. Difficulties are just part of life, so let's learn how to get through them and not let them stop us.

Remember, the rain falls on the just and the unjust. (Matthew 5:45) Disappointments and difficulties are just a part of life.

> But as they sailed He fell asleep. And a windstorm came down on the lake, and they were filling with water, and were in jeopardy. And they came to Him and awoke Him, saying, "Master, Master, we are perishing!" Then He arose and rebuked the wind and the raging of the water. And

Keys to Overcoming Part I
Overcoming Life's Disappointments & Difficulties Part I

> they ceased, and there was a calm. But He said to them, "Where is your faith?" ...
> Luke 8:23-25

In this situation Jesus was demonstrating to His disciples that He had power and authority over every situation in life. If we put our faith and trust in Jesus, He will be there for us no matter how difficult or distressing the situations we face seem to be. This is the question I want to ask you today, "Where is your faith in relationship to all that you are going through? Have you reached the point where you can't take it anymore?"

Life Situations That Try Our Faith

What kind of situations and trials are trying your faith and seem insurmountable in your eyes?

Broken relationships	**Financial problems**
Busy lifestyle	**God's chastening**
Divine delay in God's promises	**A death**
Emotional problems	**Marital problems**
Family problems, children, etc.	**Sickness**

In each of these areas we are susceptible to disappointment, difficulty and heartache. Where is your faith in each of these areas? Jesus has given us authority and power over all the issues of life. He wants us to be overcomers in all that we do and in all that comes our way.

> "These things I have spoken to you, that in Me you may have peace. In the world you will have tribulation; but be of good cheer, I have overcome the world."
> John 16:33

Keys to Overcoming Part I
Overcoming Life's Disappointments & Difficulties Part I

The problem is that we have an enemy who wants to exploit the areas in our lives that are causing us heartache, disappointment and difficulty.

Satan's Objective Is To Wear Us Down

The scriptures talk about the Antichrist, which will be released in the earth in the last days prior to Christ's coming. But it is important to know that the spirit of antichrist is already loose and working toward these same objectives. (1 John 2:18)

The antichrist spirit that is loose in the world today is trying to wear God's precious saints out with discouragement in the mist of the various trials and hardships of life (Daniel 7:25). His approach is to plant the seeds of apostasy so that when the time comes we will not have any faith to draw upon. His objective is to get as many saints as possible to lose heart and faith which will lead to apostasy. He wants to take as many down with him as he possibly can. The Bible tells us we are not to be ignorant of his devices.

> ...lest Satan should take advantage of us; for we are not ignorant of his devices.
> 2 Corinthians 2:11

Satan Feeds On Our Vulnerabilities

> Now when the devil had ended every temptation, he departed from Him until an opportune time.
> Luke 4:13

We know that Satan feeds on our weaknesses and delights in exploiting our vulnerable points, so let's look at these areas once again that have the potential of bringing weariness to our lives. These are all common causes of discouragement that make us weary in well doing.

Keys to Overcoming Part I
Overcoming Life's Disappointments & Difficulties Part I

Broken relationships	**Financial problems**
Busy lifestyle	**God's chastening**
Divine delay in God's promises	**A death**
Emotional problems	**Marital problems**
Family problems, children, etc.	**Sickness or health**

Do you feel in jeopardy in any of these areas? If so, God will give you the strength to fight and win in every situation. He has a shield just for you that fits your every need. It's called the shield of faith! As you identify the area where you are vulnerable use the shield of faith and the belt of truth against it. Satan is firing his fiery darts, so you'd better get your shield up to protect yourself.

> Therefore take up the whole armor of God, that you may be able to withstand in the evil day, and having done all, to stand. Stand therefore, having girded your waist with truth, having put on the breastplate of righteousness, and having shod your feet with the preparation of the gospel of peace; above all, taking the shield of faith with which you will be able to quench all the fiery darts of the wicked one.
> Ephesians 6:13-16

devo 3

Keys to Overcoming
Part II

**Overcoming Life's Disappointments & Difficulties
Part II**

In the last devotional, I shared with you about having the kind of faith that is able to overcome life's disappointments and difficulties. When we learn how to face all of life's situations correctly and with God's direction, we can have a hope that will get us through anything. I shared with you how Satan has access to us and how he fights us. Today is how to apply the shield of faith.

Remember, the rain falls on the just and the unjust (Matthew 5:45). Disappointments and difficulties are just part of life.

How To Apply The Shield Of Faith

> Therefore take up the whole armor of God, that you may be able to withstand in the evil day, and having done all, to stand. Stand therefore, having girded your waist with truth, having put on the

Keys to Overcoming Part II
Overcoming Life's Disappointments & Difficulties Part II

> breastplate of righteousness, and having shod your feet with the preparation of the gospel of peace; above all, taking the shield of faith with which you will be able to quench all the fiery darts of the wicked one.
> Ephesians 6:13-16

Now that we understand that we have a vicious and unrelenting enemy who is out to get us and to wear us down, what are some practical ways in which we can apply the shield of faith against him?

Know That God Wants to Take Us from Trial to Victory

> For whatever is born of God overcomes the world. And this is the victory that has overcome the world; our faith.
> 1 John 5:4

Understand The Source of Your Faith

> ...looking unto Jesus, the author and finisher of our faith, who for the joy that was set before Him endured the cross, despising the shame, and has sat down at the right hand of the throne of God.
> Hebrews 12:2

The source of our faith is Jesus Christ and what He has done for us. He is the Author and Finisher of our faith and will always be on our side no matter what. Many times when we are in life's hardest trials, the accuser of the brethren comes to us and tries to convince us that we are unworthy of God's help in our lives. This is a lie to prevent us from receiving the help we really need.

Keys to Overcoming Part II
Overcoming Life's Disappointments & Difficulties Part II

You've got to know the truth that if God is for you, who can be against you (Romans 8:31)!

> But now, thus says the LORD, who created you, O Jacob, and He who formed you, O Israel: "Fear not, for I have redeemed you; I have called you by your name; you are Mine. When you pass through the waters, I will be with you; and through the rivers, they shall not overflow you. When you walk through the fire, you shall not be burned, nor shall the flame scorch you."
> Isaiah 43:1-2

> But those who wait on the LORD shall renew their strength; they shall mount up with wings like eagles, they shall run and not be weary, they shall walk and not faint.
> Isaiah 40:31

There were many Bible characters, which for one reason or another became weary and despondent over their situation in life, but in the end became overcomers because they knew where their faith was.

We not only have the shield of faith to protect us from Satan's lies, but we can also apply the belt of truth and the sword of the Spirit from our spiritual arsenal.

> Your testimonies also are my delight And my counselors. My soul clings to the dust; revive me according to Your word.
> Psalm 119:24-25

Everyone has hard times and we can extend the misery of the situation in our lives when we don't apply the word of God to the

Keys to Overcoming Part II
Overcoming Life's Disappointments & Difficulties Part II

situation. On the other hand, when the Word of God is applied it will begin to change things. We must take the word of God and apply it to the situation that is bringing distress in our lives no matter how weak or lethargic we feel.

> So then faith comes by hearing, and hearing by the word of God.
> Romans 10:17

Job probably experienced as much hardship and disappointment as anyone and his testimony was of counting God's word as more valuable than food itself.

> My foot has held fast to His steps; I have kept His way and not turned aside. I have not departed from the commandment of His lips; I have treasured the words of His mouth more than my necessary food.
> Job 23:11-12

Find God's Purpose & Build Christlike Character in Your Life

> And we know that all things work together for good to those who love God, to those who are the called according to His purpose.
> Romans 8:28

The tough times we go through represent opportunities for God's purpose to come out of our lives. They are opportunities to build godly character in our lives. When we approach these situations with a God mentality and a heart of faith, God is able to bring joy right into the center of the difficulty. The joy of the

Keys to Overcoming Part II
Overcoming Life's Disappointments & Difficulties Part II

Lord is our strength, which counteracts Satan's tactic of wearing us down.

> And not only that, but we also glory in tribulations, knowing that tribulation produces perseverance; and perseverance, character; and character, hope.
> Romans 5:3-4

> My brethren, count it all joy when you fall into various trials, knowing that the testing of your faith produces patience. But let patience have its perfect work, that you may be perfect and complete, lacking nothing.
> James 1:2-4

> Though I walk in the midst of trouble, You will revive me; You will stretch out Your hand Against the wrath of my enemies, And Your right hand will save me. The LORD will perfect that which concerns me; Your mercy, O LORD, endures forever; Do not forsake the works of Your hands.
> Psalm 138:7-8

> And my God shall supply all your need according to His riches in glory by Christ Jesus.
> Philippians 4:19

These are some basic steps to overcoming life's disappointments and difficulties which you will surely experience from time to time.

If you allow God to work His purpose in your life by going to Him and His word during the time of difficulty you will find

Keys to Overcoming Part II
Overcoming Life's Disappointments & Difficulties Part II

yourself in a place of contentment. When you are able to find contentment, the shield of faith not only causes Satan to leave you alone, but it will release God's hand of provision in your trial.

> And let us not grow weary while doing good, for in due season we shall reap if we do not lose heart.
> Galatians 6:9

devo 4

Keys to Determination

DETERMINATION - Making the Determined Effort!

Determination is a necessary part of our spiritual walk with the Lord. You can have plenty of vision, insight and purpose, but without determination you will not get the job done. When your vision and purpose fail, your determination must kick in to keep you going in the midst of doubt and uncertainty.

> Keep your heart with all diligence, for out of it spring the issues of life. Put away from you a deceitful mouth, and put perverse lips far from you. Let your eyes look straight ahead, and your eyelids look right before you. Ponder the path of your feet, and let all your ways be established. Do not turn to the right or the left; remove your foot from evil.
> Proverbs 4:23-27

Keys to Determination
DETERMINATION - Making the Determined Effort!

- Determination is inner fortitude and strength of character.
- Disciplined to remain consistent, strong and diligent despite the odds or the demands.
- The act of deciding definitely and firmly, or coming to a resolve.
- Determination is acting in faith when we temporarily lose sight of where we are going.

Determination Is an <u>Important</u> Part of Our Spiritual Warfare

> Watch, stand fast in the faith, be brave, be strong.
> 1 Corinthians 16:13

> Therefore take up the whole armor of God, that you may be able to withstand in the evil day, and having done all, to stand.
> Ephesians 6:13

The Example of <u>Manasseh</u> and the Canaanites

God had given all of the tribes of Israel the command to go into the Promised Land and to drive out all of its inhabitants. He not only commanded them, He promised them that He would help them. They had vision, purpose and destiny, but did they have the determination needed to possess all that God had given to them?

> "Have I not commanded you? Be strong and of good courage; do not be afraid, nor be dismayed, for the LORD your God is with you wherever you go."
> Joshua 1:9

With this promise and destiny, the children of Israel were to conquer all of the inhabitants of the Promised Land. We find

Keys to Determination
DETERMINATION - Making the Determined Effort!

however, that this did not happen in all cases, because of the determination of their enemies to continue to dwell in the land.

> Yet the children of Manasseh could not drive out the inhabitants of those cities, but the Canaanites were determined to dwell in that land. And it happened, when the children of Israel grew strong, that they put the Canaanites to forced labor, but did not utterly drive them out.
> Joshua 17:12-13

The reason the children of Manasseh were not able to drive the Canaanites completely out of the land was because they lacked the determination to do so. The Canaanites were more determined to stay than the Tribe of Manasseh was determined to drive them out.

Through a Determined Effort, We Are to <u>Drive</u> Out Our Enemies.

How many of us allow strongholds to remain in our lives, because we lack the determination to completely drive them out? God has given us the authority and the power to destroy things that are holding us captive.

> Behold, I give you the authority to trample on serpents and scorpions, and over all the power of the enemy, and nothing shall by any means hurt you.
> Luke 10:19

We all have strongholds in our lives that our enemy is trying to hold onto with a determined effort. The thing that we have to realize is that we must have a more determined effort than the

Keys to Determination
DETERMINATION - Making the Determined Effort!

enemy, realizing that *greater is He who is in us than he who is in the world.*

> You are of God, little children, and have overcome them, because He who is in you is greater than he who is in the world.
> 1 John 4:4

Your enemy won't give up that easily. He is determined, so therefore you must realize that it takes a determined effort on your part to defeat him. We are wrestling against principalities, against powers, against rulers of the darkness of this age, against spiritual hosts of wickedness in the heavenly places.

> For we do not wrestle against flesh and blood, but against principalities, against powers, against the rulers of the darkness of this age, against spiritual hosts of wickedness in the heavenly places. Therefore take up the whole armor of God, that you may be able to withstand in the evil day, and having done all, to stand.
> Ephesians 6:12-13

Many Christians fail in many areas because of failure to make THE determined effort. Marriages, children, jobs, business, ministry, sin, and our prayer life are areas that our enemy wants to continue to hold onto. Are you letting him, simply because he is more determined than you are?

Do you have the inner fortitude and strength of character to remain consistent, strong and diligent regardless of the odds or the demands that are being placed upon you in these areas?

> Be sober, be vigilant; because your adversary the devil walks about like a roaring lion, seeking

Keys to Determination
DETERMINATION - Making the Determined Effort!

> whom he may devour. Resist him, **steadfast in the faith,** knowing that the same sufferings are experienced by your brotherhood in the world.
> 1 Peter 5:8-9 Emphasis added

DETERMINATION HELPS US CROSS THE FINISH LINE!

When we experience defeats, setbacks, discouragements and other hindrances, we must be like the apostle Paul who said, *"None of these things move me."*

> But none of these things move me; nor do I count my life dear to myself, so that I may finish my race with joy, and the ministry which I received from the Lord Jesus, to testify to the gospel of the grace of God.
> Acts 20:24

A page from John Wesley's Diary reads as follows:

- Sunday am, May 5, preached in St. Ann's; was asked not to come back anymore.
- Sunday pm, May 5, preached at St. John's; deacons said, "Get out and stay out."
- Sunday am, May 12 preached at St. Jude's; can't go back there either.
- Sunday pm, May 12 preached at St. George's; kicked out again.
- Sunday am, May 19 preached at St. somebody else's; deacons called special meeting and said I couldn't return.
- Sunday pm, May 19 preached on the street; kicked off the street.
- Sunday am, May 26 preached in meadow; chased out of meadow as a bull was turned loose during the services.

Keys to Determination
DETERMINATION - Making the Determined Effort!

- Sunday am, June 2   preached out at the edge of town; kicked off the highway.
- Sunday pm, June 2   afternoon service, preached in a pasture; 10,000 people came to hear me and were saved.

Without determination we will find ourselves being tossed here and there and beaten to a pulp when challenges come against us. When the pressure is on we will find ourselves reacting in a way that is contradictory to what we believe. We must have the inner fortitude and strength of character to remain consistent, strong and diligent regardless of the odds or the demands.

My prayer is that you would come to the place in your life where you have more determination than the enemy in dealing with your issues and moving forward in faith towards the destiny God has for you.

devo 5

Keys to Flavor Your World

Being a Christian in a Non-Christian World

We live in a world that presents many challenges to our faith and we must be able to overcome and cope in such a way that shows and proves that greater is He who is within us than he who is in the world. (1Joun 4:4)

We must maintain Christlike attitudes in a world that is heavily influenced by the evil one and all of his evil attitudes and devices.

> We know that we are of God, and the whole world lies under the sway of the wicked one.
> 1 John 5:19

When it says the whole world lies under the sway of the wicked one, it means the world is under the controlling influence

Keys to Flavor Your World
Being a Christian in a Non-Christian World

of the devil. It means the devil, or the wicked one, is using all of his ability to exercise influence and authority.

Jesus warned us of these attitudes and Paul warned Timothy in his letter to him. We find many passages in the Bible that give us a good idea of the kind of attitudes that are being promoted and influenced in today's world with much authority.

> And because lawlessness will abound, the love of many will grow cold.
> Matthew 24:12

> But know this, that in the last days perilous times will come: For men will be lovers of themselves, lovers of money, boasters, proud, blasphemers, disobedient to parents, unthankful, unholy, unloving, unforgiving, slanderers, without self-control, brutal, despisers of good, traitors, headstrong, haughty, lovers of pleasure rather than lovers of God, having a form of godliness but denying its power. And from such people turn away!
> 2 Timothy 3:1-5

These are many of the attitudes that Christians have to deal with and contend with every day of their lives. They are also attitudes that are promoted heavily through the media.

If the world were full of godly characteristics, wouldn't it be easier for us to put on the wonderful characteristics of Christ's nature? But it is not, and that makes it much harder to put on the clothing that belongs to the Lord Jesus Christ. The world hates those attitudes.

> If you were of the world, the world would love its own. Yet because you are not of the world, but I

Keys to Flavor Your World
Being a Christian in a Non-Christian World

> chose you out of the world, therefore the world hates you.
> John 15:19

> I have given them Your word; and the world has hated them because they are not of the world, just as I am not of the world.
> John 17:14

The Challenge for Christians in Today's World.

1. DON'T BE A COMPLAINER!

> Do all things without complaining and disputing, that you may become blameless and harmless, children of God without fault in the midst of a crooked and perverse generation, among whom you shine as lights in the world, holding fast the word of life, so that I may rejoice in the day of Christ that I have not run in vain or labored in vain.
> Philippians 2:14-16

> Pure and undefiled religion before God and the Father is this: to visit orphans and widows in their trouble, and to keep oneself unspotted from the world.
> James 1:27

This means that we cannot afford to allow our attitudes and characteristics to be molded by the world. We are called to resist the mold of the world.

Keys to Flavor Your World
Being a Christian in a Non-Christian World

> And do not be conformed to this world, but be transformed by the renewing of your mind, that you may prove what is that good and acceptable and perfect will of God.
> Romans 12:2

2. HAVE GOOD FLAVOR!

Do you taste good as a Christian? Our calling and destiny as Christians is to be salt and light of the world in which we find ourselves.

> You are the salt of the earth; but if the salt loses its flavor, how shall it be seasoned? It is then good for nothing but to be thrown out and trampled underfoot by men. You are the light of the world. A city that is set on a hill cannot be hidden.
> Matthew 5:13-14

What this Scripture is encouraging us to do, is to be the controlling influence in the world.

In order to be the kind of controlling influence in the world that God has called us to be will mean that each one of us takes on the responsibility of putting on the Lord Jesus Christ and all of His garments. As we do this we truly become salt and light and are able to act as a preserving agent and begin to flavor the world around us.

devo 6

Keys to Values

The Importance of VALUES

There are many issues that are relevant to the changing times in which we live. How do we as Christians contend with the changing values that our culture is going through? Being in a world whose values are constantly changing makes it more difficult and complex to live in harmony with God's plan and purpose.

The chart below shows how cultural values changed.

1950's	2000's
Saving	Spending
Delayed gratification	Instant Gratification
Ozzie and Harriet	Latchkey Kids
Certainty	Ambivalence
Orthodoxy	Skepticism
Investing	Leveraging
Neighborhood	Lifestyle
Middle Class	Under Class
Export	Import

Keys to Values
The Importance of VALUES

Public Virtue	Personal Well-being
Mom & Dad	Nanny and Day Care
Press Conference	Photo Opportunity
Achievement	Fame
Knowledge	Credential
Duty	Divorce
"We"	"Me"

These present day values are a fulfillment of the Apostle Paul's prophecy concerning the last days, when he said, *"Men shall be lovers of self, unholy, lovers of money and without self-control."*

> But know this, that in the last days perilous times will come: For men will be lovers of themselves, lovers of money, boasters, proud, blasphemers, disobedient to parents, unthankful, unholy, unloving, unforgiving, slanderers, without self-control, brutal, despisers of good,
> 2 Timothy 3:1-3

Aside from all of these areas, we are also living in an era when evil is being called good and good is being called evil. Sin is running rampant in our culture and society, which is why the values and morality of our culture are deteriorating before our eyes.

> Woe to those who call evil good, and good evil;
> Who put darkness for light, and light for darkness;
> Who put bitter for sweet, and sweet for bitter!
> Isaiah 5:20

As an example of how much our values have changed, think back to the year 1939. That was the year the movie *Gone with the Wind* was released, including in its script a scandal-making four

Keys to Values
The Importance of VALUES

letter word that raised the eyebrows of movie goers around the world. Has there been much of a change since 1939? Do four letter words still create scandals? What a joke!

In the last several years we have seen television shows such as Ophra, Geraldo, Jerry Springer and others parade just about every kind of perversion you can think of before our eyes. They have centered on personalities and adventures of subnormal and abnormal people – prostitutes, mistresses, criminals, the emotionally deranged, hate groups and other social derelicts. The sex adventures of urbanized cavemen and rapists, the lives of adulterers, fornicators, playboys and entertainment personalities are all paraded before the public to accept.

Porno shops are now in every major American city. Hard core XXX-rated films are now available on pay cable television as well as in hotels. We have reached an all-time low with "kiddie porn." Even prime time TV isn't exempt from intimate bedroom scenes, verbal explosions of profanity, and a rather frequent diet of so called humor regarding sexual intercourse, homosexuality, nudity, and various parts of the human anatomy. We've drifted a long way since 1939.

As we can see, our cultural values have changed over the years. They have been eroding steadily and will probably continue to do so. The question is, how do we as Christians contend with these changing values? How do we keep from becoming desensitized? How do we keep our values simple and Biblical in today's complex world? How do we overcome in a world that has gone awry?

Is Christianity Still The Champion of Godly Values?

We should ask ourselves this question, "Is Christianity still the champion of purity and godly values or are we being swept along in the tide of cultural change as well? Does Christianity still have the punch that it had twenty to twenty five years ago in the realm of purity and values?"

Keys to Values
The Importance of VALUES

It's not that Christianity has begun to lose its punch over the past twenty to twenty five years; it seems that more and more Christians are either compromising or opting for lower standards when confronted with the choice of living in moral purity as set forth in the Scriptures.

The battle of choices is not new.

Two sections of the New Testament, written in the first century describe the internal warfare quite vividly.

> knowing this, that our old man was crucified with Him, that the body of sin might be done away with, that we should no longer be slaves of sin.
> Romans 6:6

> Therefore do not let sin reign in your mortal body, that you should obey it in its lusts. And do not present your members as instruments of unrighteousness to sin, but present yourselves to God as being alive from the dead, and your members as instruments of righteousness to God.
> Romans 6:12-13

> For the flesh lusts against the Spirit, and the Spirit against the flesh; and these are contrary to one another, so that you do not do the things that you wish.
> Galatians 5:17

Yes, Christianity is still the champion of purity and morality, but the challenges and attacks against purity and morality have never been greater, complicating the problem and making it more complex for us.

devo 7

Keys to Changing Values

How To Contend With Changing Values

We Must Believe the Values Given in God's Word are Still Relevant in Today's Culture

> Forever, O LORD, Your word is settled in heaven.
> Psalms 119:89
>
> Your word is a lamp to my feet And a light to my path.
> Psalms 119:105
>
> All Scripture is given by inspiration of God, and is profitable for doctrine, for reproof, for correction, for instruction in righteousness,
> 2 Timothy 3:16

There are those who say, "The Bible and its values and standards are outdated. We live in a progressive culture; The

Keys to Changing Values
How To Contend With Changing Values

Bible is no longer relevant to the society in which we live." The answer to that comment is simple. As the writer of Ecclesiastes said, "There is nothing new under the sun." There have been ancient cultures that have been just as corrupt as our culture. It was in the midst of some of these cultures that God's word came forth.

> That which has been is what will be, That which is done is what will be done, And there is nothing new under the sun. Is there anything of which it may be said, "See, this is new"? It has already been in ancient times before us.
> Ecclesiastes 1:9-10

Throughout the generations of time people have continuously moved through cycles. Nothing is new. Clothing styles are an example of this.

Our values and morals are molded by our belief system. If our belief system begins to decay, so will our morals. This is what has happened in our culture. As Christians we must come to a firm belief in and adherence to God's word and its relevance for our lives.

For Christianity to retain its role as "the champion of purity," the Christian is expected to be above reproach. The same is as true today as it was in the first century.

> that you may become blameless and harmless, children of God without fault in the midst of a crooked and perverse generation, among whom you shine as lights in the world, holding fast the word of life, so that I may rejoice in the day of Christ that I have not run in vain or labored in vain.
> Philippians 2:15-16

Keys to Changing Values
How To Contend With Changing Values

We must Determine Values That Are Not So Black and White

There are many areas in which our societal values have simply become immoral and evil according to God's Word, but there are other areas in which values have simply shifted to more self-serving and self-pleasing. As Christians we are often able to discern when something is outright wrong and evil and is being promoted as good, but what about values that have become more self gratifying? How do we discern and make right choices when society's values are constantly shifting and changing?

We Must Consider The Consequences

Living right morally means living in ways that bring good things to people. Is my decision going to hurt them or help them? What really matters morally is whether we are adding to the goodness of people's lives.

> Let nothing be done through selfish ambition or conceit, but in lowliness of mind let each esteem others better than himself. Let each of you look out not only for his own interests, but also for the interests of others.
> Philippians 2:3-4

We must Choose to Live in the Beneficial Realm of God's Grace Rather than the Permissible

> You say, "I am allowed to do anything"—but not everything is good for you. You say, "I am allowed to do anything"—but not everything is beneficial. Don't be concerned for your own good but for the good of others.
> 1 Corinthians 10:23-24 (NLT)

Keys to Changing Values
How To Contend With Changing Values

Knowing and Practicing God's Word Gives Us Discernment.

> For someone who lives on milk is still an infant and doesn't know how to do what is right. Solid food is for those who are mature, who through training have the skill to recognize the difference between right and wrong.
> Hebrews 5:13-14 (NLT)

The more we adhere to and practice God's Word in our lives, the more we develop the ability to discern the appropriate response in the many different situations that come up in our lives.

Discernment is often simply being awake and having a nose for what is going on beneath the surface, and having a sense for the more fitting response to it. This is what makes for a class act on the moral stage.

But like everything else, discernment takes practice; it doesn't come easily. It is a gift, and like all personal gifts it comes only with exercise. It is not a gut reaction; it comes with using our eyes, our ears, our minds, our imaginations, our empathy and, yes, our intuition.

Discernment can be one of the most essential tools that we have when it comes to making good value judgments. What we have to be careful about is editing out the segments of reality that will cost us something. We have a tendency to whittle and chisel reality into nice shapes that fit our needs. We abridge our consciousness to protect ourselves.

- America's Founding Fathers declared that all people are created equal, but some of them screened out of their own consciousness the reality of thousands of black people living without freedom before their eyes.

Keys to Changing Values
How To Contend With Changing Values

- German citizens refused to discern the reality of Jewish people disappearing from their neighborhoods and villages, and thus refused to know that the Holocaust was happening just around the corner.
- A suburban mother refused to see the clear signs that her son was taking drugs; it would be too painful to let the reality inside her consciousness.

Because of our sensitivity to pain we distort the reality around us and we cannot give genuine responses to what is really going on and as a result we make wrong moral decisions.

Do My Decisions Support My Commitments?
When responsible people make a decision, they ask themselves, *"How will it impact my significant commitments?"* Sometimes the answer is clear, definite, certain. Can selling military secrets to the enemy ever support your commitment to your country? Can having an affair with someone else's spouse ever support your commitment to your own marriage? Can telling your friend's secrets to a third party ever support your commitment to your friendship? Will you undermine your commitment to your family if you take on an extra job?

As we can see, we are living in an era in which values are constantly changing. But God's Word never changes, nor do His values. If we purpose to live our lives in accordance with His Word we will escape the corruption that is in this world. Christianity is still the champion of godly values!

Forever, O LORD, **Your word** is settled in heaven.
Psalms 119:89 Emphasis added

devo 8

Keys to Overcoming Fear

500 Fears — You Can Overcome Them!

Did you know there or over 500 fears with a name? **Clinically:** *A phobia is a type of anxiety disorder. It is a strong, irrational fear of something that poses little or no actual danger.* **Spiritually / Biblically:** *A phobia is a spirit and its purpose is to limit you, hinder you, blind you, stop you.*

> Let your conduct be without covetousness; be content with such things as you have. For He Himself has said, "I will never leave you nor forsake you." So we may boldly say: "The LORD is my helper; I will not **fear**. What can man do to me?:"
> Hebrews 13:5-6 Emphasis added

It's been said, **"The best way to overcome a fear of something is to stare it straight in the face."**

Keys to Overcoming Fear
500 Fears — You Can Overcome Them!

... call to remembrance the genuine faith that is in you, which dwelt first in your grandmother Lois and your mother Eunice, and I am persuaded is in you also. Therefore I remind you to stir up the gift of God which is in you through the laying on of my hands. For God has not given us a **spirit of fear**, but of power and of love and of a sound mind. Therefore do not be ashamed of the testimony of our Lord, nor of me His prisoner, but share with me in the sufferings for the gospel according to the power of God,
2 Timothy 1:5-8 Emphasis added

Whoever shall confess that Jesus is the Son of God, God dwells in him and he in God. And we have known and believed the love that God has in us. God is love, and he who abides in love abides in God, and God in him. In this is our love made perfect, that we may have boldness in the day of judgment, that as He is, so are we in this world. There is no fear in **love**, but perfect **love** casts out fear, because fear has torment. He who fears has not been perfected in **love**.
1 John 4:15-18 Emphasis added

I'm not going to attempt to name every fear (as I can't even pronounce some of them), but I do want to address two fears that face us more than any when moving into our purpose and calling in life:

First — **FEAR OF SUCCESS**
Fear of success is the fear of accomplishment and being recognized and honored; Belief that no matter how much you are able to achieve or accomplish, it will never be enough to sustain

Keys to Overcoming Fear
500 Fears — You Can Overcome Them!

success. **EVERYONE has a fear of something in life.** But there's no reason to fear the good stuff.

4 Reasons Why People Have A Fear Of Success

REASON #1: "I'm not worth it. I don't deserve it"
This problem is the biggie. You must be honest enough with yourself to admit that you do have a challenge with your self worth! There are many other reasons for fear of success caused by a crummy self-image. One of them is a lack of belief in your own ability to sustain progress, and maintain the spiritual momentum in your life; the belief that there are others out there who are better and smarter than you, who will replace or displace you (and let me tell you that you are RIGHT! There ARE people better and smarter than you and there always will be, but there are also millions of people who don't hold a candle to you)!

> For a great and effective door has opened to me, and there are many adversaries. Now if Timothy comes, see that he may be with you without **fear**; for he does the work of the Lord, as I also do. Therefore let no one despise him. But send him on his journey in peace, that he may come to me; for I am waiting for him with the brethren.
> 1 Corinthians 16:9-11 Emphasis added

REASON #2: "If I achieve the calling on my life I won't be who I am."
Very often people are afraid that if they reach their goal they will have to stop being who they are and start playing someone else's role. TRUTH— if you don't walk out your purpose, you will have to change your personality or your wrong personality will change you.

Keys to Overcoming Fear
500 Fears — You Can Overcome Them!

> What the wicked fears will come upon him; but the desire of the righteous will be granted.
> Proverbs 10:24 (NASB)

You must realize that you will have to change. Life is a constant motion, a constant change. That's what keeps us growing, moving forward, getting rid of the obstacles that slow us down. Success is often tied to all kinds of weird beliefs and fears that have been squished into our minds. But the fact is that achievement is something that is very good indeed!

REASON #3: "It is impossible!"
QUESTION: What can you do if you don't believe it is possible?
- *"For with God, all things are possible to him that believes" (Matthew 10:27, Mark 9:23)*
- *"If someone else has done it, so can I!"*
- *"Greater is He that is in you then he that is in the world!:" (1 John 4:4)*

Achievement isn't science– it's FAITH. You just have to free that great thinker, great winner, great fighter, GREATER SPIRIT IN YOU. I want you to realize that it is not a question of the actual possibility or impossibility of your goal. It is your personal FAITH.

REASON #4: "I can't do it!"
It literally means, "I don't know how to do it" ... sometimes; "It requires too much practice to get good at 'it' so I can't do it."... And most of the time it worked! "If I can't do it, it is meant to be this way." What would happen... if, for a day, you believed that you CAN do it as strongly as you believed you can't? Now that's an interesting thought; problem is, in that day you'd probably get over the hump and do it.

Keys to Overcoming Fear
500 Fears — You Can Overcome Them!

Second — **FEAR OF FAILURE**

Fear of failure is the fear of making mistakes and losing approval; fear that your accomplishments can self-destruct at anytime; being afraid you're going to lose it all. Remember:

> What the wicked fears shall come upon him; but the desire of the righteous will be granted.
> Proverbs 10:24 (NASB)

> and most of the brethren in the Lord, having become confident by my chains, are much more bold to speak the word without **fear**.
> Philippians 1:14 Emphasis added

How to Face the Fear of Failure:

Step #1: Take action. Take bold, decisive action! Do something scary! Fear of failure immobilizes you. To overcome this fear, you must act. When you act, act boldly. "What would you do if you knew you could not fail?" What could you achieve? Be brave and just do it. If it doesn't work out the way you want, then do something else. But DO SOMETHING NOW.

Step #2 Persist. Successful people just don't give up. They keep trying different approaches to achieving their outcomes until they finally get the results they want.

Step #3: Don't take failure personally. Failure is about behavior, outcomes, and results. Failure is not a personality characteristic. Because you made a mistake, doesn't mean that you are a failure.

Step #4: Do things differently. If what you are doing isn't working, do something else. There is an old saying,

Keys to Overcoming Fear
500 Fears — You Can Overcome Them!

- "If you always do what you've always done, you'll always get what you always got."
- If you're not getting the results you want, then you must do something different. Many people stop doing anything at all, and this guarantees they won't be successful.

Step #5: Don't be so hard on yourself. Hey, at least you know what doesn't work. Look at failure as an event or a happening, not as a person.

Step #6: Treat the experience as an opportunity to learn. Think of failure as a learning experience. What did you learn from the experience that will help you in the future? Use what you learned from the experience to do things differently so you get different results next time. Learn from the experience, or ignore it.

Step #7: Fail forward fast. Tom Peters, "the management guru," says that in today's business world, companies must fail forward fast. What he means is that the way we learn is by making mistakes. So if we want to learn at a faster pace, we must make mistakes at a faster pace. The key is that you must learn from the mistakes you make so you don't repeat them.

ONE LAST THING...
REMEMBER– THE OPPOSITE OF FEAR IS FAITH. I challenge you to build your faith and conquer your fears. BELOW ARE SOME GREAT FAITH SCRIPTURES!

> Watch, stand fast in the **faith**, be brave, be strong.
> 1 Corinthians 16:13 Emphasis added

> For we walk by **faith**, not by sight.
> 2Corinthians 5:7 Emphasis added

Keys to Overcoming Fear
500 Fears — You Can Overcome Them!

But without **faith** it is impossible to please Him, for he who comes to God must believe that He is and that He is a rewarder of those who diligently seek Him.
Hebrews 11:6 Emphasis added

devo 9

Keys to Keeping a Marriage

What Really Keeps a Marriage Together?

As a pastor and mentor, I have sat down with many men and had the conversation about the failure of their marriage. Some have been in their thirties and some into their sixties. After pain and failure and on their last leg before the divorce, many of them are relieved that this painful experience is almost over, while at the same time being very sad, grieving that the marriage they wanted to have never happened—living in the shattered dream of the life that he wishes they could have had together. It's good in one way that they feel like this, because it tells me they are dealing with divorce in a healthy manner. I never trust anyone if they tell me they have no sadness about their marriage ending and that they are simply glad that it is over. Marriages are investments and we are always sad when an investment goes belly up.

Most of the time, people in this situation never take the time to ask the right question until it's too late. I know God can restore

Keys to Keeping a Marriage
What Really Keeps a Marriage Together?

love and passion and there can be new life brought into a marriage. I've seen restoration many times; however, I have seen the sadness of broken relationships as well. So what's the right question to ask? What if there was a desperate plea for the right answer before it was too late? What is that question we all should be asking about our marriages? What "type" of love keeps a marriage together? Before you answer too quickly, think about the kind of love that can keep a marriage relationship glued together for life. As I meditated on this for a while, here is my conclusion.

Having considered my own marriage, the countless couples I have seen as a pastor, messages I've preached and heard in the Church, what my upbringing taught me as well as the dozens of books I've read on the subject over the years, I believe the key is simply this....

First, I used to think that *agape* was the most important kind of love for a marriage. But, after seeing some very spiritual people grow distant, I no longer think it's the key. This Greek word suggests that a spiritual love is the number one priority—a love that is sacrificial and focused on commitment more than feelings or your own needs. After all, haven't we all heard more sermons than we could count where this was the bottom line?

Don't get me wrong agape is very important in keeping a marriage together. But it's not the "most" important kind of love. Many couples have intact marriages but no relationship at all and are living under the stoic belief that happiness isn't even a possibility.

Secondly, *eros* is really wonderful, but it doesn't "keep" a marriage together either. We all love passion. We love it when we can get what makes us feel good. We all want there to be chemistry. We all dream about great sex that will keep us interested over the years. Our culture is so sex obsessed that we are easily convinced (especially early in a marriage) that the

Keys to Keeping a Marriage
What Really Keeps a Marriage Together?

lucky ones can't stay out of the bedroom; that this is the secret to a long relationship.

Don't get me wrong, "feeling" in love with your partner is very critical. Too many accept a relationship that is boring and no longer has any passion. Eros (in the right sense of the word) can be restored and must be worked at over the life of a marriage.

Based on my marriage, and the successful ones I've seen over the years, I have come to the conclusion that *phileo* is most important. Commitment and chemistry are ingredients you don't want to leave out of the recipe but **without friendship** you can't have the marriage you were meant to have!

To be friends with your mate means:
- You respect her.
- You treat her like your equal when your upbringing and your own selfish ways try to convince you otherwise.
- You talk about how you feel and think about the good and bad of your life together.
- You even risk conflict by being more honest than you are comfortable with because it builds intimacy into your marriage.
- You plan and dream together because life is too complicated to just wing it.

In other words, you treat your partner like your "best" friend.

Sadly, so many marriages never have this between spouses – *friendship.* People have not been told it's the most important thing! In fact they may have even had the other two ingredients the majority of the time.

I hope you know this is realistic and not too pie in the sky. All I know is that I have been married over thirty five years to my best friend. Though there is not a perfect marriage out there, I thank God for my wife and I thank God for friendship!

devo 10

Keys to Remembering

10 Ways to Stop Forgetting Things & Keep Your Word!

As the father of ten I have heard the words, "I forgot," many times. Have you forgotten that thing you were supposed to do for your wife, parents, friend, or even your boss? Remember that favor you were going to do for a friend, or that tool you were going to take back that you borrowed six months ago?

How good are you at remembering what you need to do and said you would do? Do you FORGET? Do you follow through thus keeping your word that you will call back or do that task?

Here is the **spiritual reason** for not forgetting:

> "Simply let your 'Yes' be 'Yes,' and your 'No,' 'No'"
> Matthew 5:37 (NIV)

Keys to Remembering
10 Ways to Stop Forgetting Things & Keep Your Word!

The New Living Translation says it this way... *"Just say a simple, 'Yes, I will,' or 'No, I won't.'"* The last part of the verse says **"Anything beyond this comes from the evil one."**

Don't Say You Forgot
    Your word is at stake every time you commit to doing something for someone. One of the all time worst excuses, beside "I don't have time," is, *"I was going to do it... But, I forgot." Wow, have I heard that before!*
    Are you guilty of saying that you are going to do something and then didn't because you forgot? Forgetting is not an excuse; it is a *root cause* of productivity issues. Whether it is to-dos, appointments, obligations, or bills... forgotten tasks often cause you more work down the road.
    We all want to stay on top of our tasks and obligations. What we need are good habits and strategies to remember what we need to do.

Here are 10 Ways to Stop Forgetting & Get More Done:
- **Set an Alarm—** We all have alarm clocks on our phones, yet few of us use them. Setting an alarm is the simplest way to remind yourself.
- **Put it On Your Calendar—** Calendars are often underutilized. Don't just make appointments for meetings, but also for tasks that you need to do
- **Write it Down (on Your To-do List)—** What do you put on your to-do list? Many people only write down the *big* things. Ironically, the big things are usually pretty easy to remember. My list is full of the small things I am likely to forget.
- **Set a Reminder—** Alarms are great for one-of's. However, for regular or repeating tasks go ahead and set a reminder. For example, I have a reminder on my iPhone that goes off every Wednesday night at 9 PM to tell me to

Keys to Remembering
10 Ways to Stop Forgetting Things & Keep Your Word!

put the trash out. I usually beat the reminder, but the few times I forgot, I was thankful.

- **Do It Now, So You Don't Have to Remember Later—** When appropriate, do small tasks right then and there. If it is only going to take a few seconds or minutes… Just Do It.
- **Have Someone Else Remind You—** Have a family member, friend, or even your wife hold you to performing a certain task.
- **Put It On Automatic—** One of my favorite ways to avoid forgetting tasks is to put them on automatic. Set and forget. This works great with Auto-Pay for bills.
- **Don't Say Yes In The First Place—** Want to avoid forgetting that favor that you promised? Or that extra task you agreed to take on? One of the best methods is to say "No" in the first place.
- **Have Someone Else Do It—** If you can't do it, delegate appropriate tasks. However, just remember that when you delegate, you still have to remember to follow up.
- **Use Your List!—** Your to-do list should be your best friend. It should remember so that you don't have to. If you are following rule #3, then your list will have your back. When your list reminds you of something you forgot, you know it's working.

devo 11

Keys to New Beginnings

Giving the New Year a Kick Start

The beginning of a New Year is a time for reevaluations and a season of new beginnings. How many times have we started a new year without realizing the goals we had previously set or even taken the time to evaluate why those goals weren't achieved?

We cannot live on yesterday's blessings and we can't live on yesterday's failures and disappointments. The new year is a time to forget the past and move forward into the present and the future.

> Brethren, I do not count myself to have apprehended; but one thing I do, forgetting those things which are behind and reaching forward to those things which are ahead, I press toward the goal for the prize of the upward call of God in Christ Jesus.
> Philippians 3:13-14

Keys to New Beginnings
Giving the New Year a Kick Start

At the beginning of each year many people all over the world make New Year's resolutions, many of which will never come to pass. This is an opportunity to look back over the past year to see if we were able to make all of the desired changes we set out to achieve.

- The beginning of a New Year can be a season of new beginnings.
- It's a time to look ahead with a sense of anticipation and excitement toward the new things God wants to do in our lives.
- It is a season of setting new goals and putting into effect those things we have been putting off.

We can look to this season as a time to reflect and reevaluate where we are and where we are going. I believe it is always God's desire that we be filled with a sense of newness and freshness of what He desires and wants to do in our lives. He greatly desires for us to be filled with a renewed sense of purpose and destiny. This is what is really needed before we can give ourselves a good kick start.

> Do not remember the former things, nor consider the things of old. Behold, I will do a new thing, now it shall spring forth; shall you not know it? I will even make a road in the wilderness and rivers in the desert.
> Isaiah 43:18-19

Over the years I have had a lot of realized goals and a lot of failures and unrealized goals as well. I've learned that we don't have to live our lives in guilt and condemnation for our failures and un-achieved goals.

Keys to New Beginnings
Giving the New Year a Kick Start

We get to wipe the slate clean and start over. God doesn't hold our past against us as long as we sincerely repent and continually press toward the goal for the prize of the upward call of God in Christ Jesus. We are a new creation in Christ every day of our lives.

> Therefore, if anyone is in Christ, he is a new creation; old things have passed away; behold, **all things** have become new.
> 2 Corinthians 5:17 Emphasis added

New things come by letting go of the past. No matter how miserably we failed in life or in our Christianity, God's desire is for us to receive His forgiveness and move forward.

> As far as the east is from the west, So far has He removed our transgressions from us.
> Psalms 103:12

Hanging on and dwelling on the past is like air moving through a dirty filter. Even though something new and fresh enters into the filter it comes out dirty and tainted because of the filth it must flow through.

One of God's principles concerning new things is to forget the past and to not walk in condemnation and guilt, but rather to walk in the freedom and the liberty of His forgiveness.

> There is therefore now no condemnation to those who are in Christ Jesus, who do not walk according to the flesh, but according to the Spirit.
> Romans 8:1

Keys to New Beginnings
Giving the New Year a Kick Start

If He has forgotten about our past sins, failures, and defeats, we must also forget and get on with the new things He desires to do in our lives.

New things come because you desire for them to come! When we get tired of the way things have been, then we are in a position to receive the new things God has prepared for us.

> Blessed are those who hunger and thirst for righteousness, For they shall be filled.
> Matthew 5:6

New things come when you let God touch your life. Get in touch with what God wants to do in your life, rather than what you want. God can only bring those new things to us when we give ourselves to Him with an open heart.

Our prayer should be for God to continually create a new heart within us and to continually renew our spirit in Him (Psalm 51:10). As we do this it will put us in the proper position for God to speak and create new things in our lives. Let the Holy Spirit reveal new things to you and allow Him to speak into your life.

> But those who wait on the LORD shall renew their strength; they shall mount up with wings like eagles, they shall run and not be weary, they shall walk and not faint.
> Isaiah 40:31

devo **12**

Keys to Change Your Year

4 Ways To Kick Start Your New Year

1. Rely on the Holy Spirit to Help You and Equip You.

> To this end **I also** labor, **striving** according to His working which works in me mightily.
> Colossians 1:29 Emphasis added

Mightily— Comes from the Greek word *dunamis, doo'-nam-is; miraculous power (by implication a miracle itself): –ability, abundance, meaning, might (-ily, -y, -y deed), (worker of) miracle (-s), power, strength, violence, mighty (wonderful) work.*

The major reason unbelievers have a hard time fulfilling their new year's resolutions is because they are doing it with their own strength.

> But if the Spirit of Him who raised Jesus from the dead dwells in you, He who raised Christ from the

Keys to Change Your Year
4 Ways To Kick Start Your New Year

> dead will also give life to your mortal bodies through His Spirit who dwells in you.
> Romans 8:11

As Christians, God has given to us the Holy Spirit and all things that pertain unto life and godliness (2 Peter 1:3). Therefore a new hope comes with new challenges and goals, because all the promises of God are yea and amen! (2 Corinthians 1:20)

2. Build on Past Successes and Learn From Past Failures.

"Great accomplishments are often attempted but only occasionally reached. Those who reach them are usually those who missed many times before. Failures are only temporary tests to prepare us for permanent triumphs." *Charles R. Swindall*

> Nevertheless, to the degree that we have already attained, let us walk by the same rule, let us be of the same mind.
> Philippians 3:16

We all have failures in our lives. It's what we do with them and how we respond to them that makes the difference. The way we deal with failure can determine how we sustain motivation.

It has been said that a successful person fails two out of every five times, while the unsuccessful person fails three out of five times. Not a whole lot of difference.

We need to look at how much we missed the mark and then make the necessary adjustments that will help us to hit the mark more perfectly in the coming year.

We should think of a goal as a target. On a target, the bull's eye is 100. Concentric rings are 80, 60, 40, and 20. You should aim for 100, but sometimes you may only hit 80 or even 20. But if you don't aim for 100, you will hit zero every time. Someone

Keys to Change Your Year
4 Ways To Kick Start Your New Year

said, "I would rather attempt to do something great for God and fail, than to do nothing and succeed."

After Dwight Eisenhower won the Republican nomination for President from Robert Taft in 1952, a reporter asked Taft about his goals. He said, "My great goal was to become President of the United States in 1953." The reporter smirked. "Well, you didn't make it, did you?" He said, "No, but I became senator from Ohio!"

3. Set New Goals.

> Where there is no revelation (*or prophetic vision – margin*), the people cast off restraint; but happy is he who keeps the law.
> Proverbs 29:18

Without vision and direction you will cast off all restraint and not fulfill those areas of change that the Lord wants to bring into your life.

What Are Your Goals for the Coming Year?

I encourage you to think about what your goals are for the coming year and then write them down.

- Make a list of areas where you want victory during this coming year.
- Make a list of areas in which you want to be more diligent.
- Make a list of new areas and experiences you want to move into.
- Make a list of new areas to which you want to commit yourself, or recommit yourself.
- Make a list of what God wants to do in your family.

Keys to Change Your Year
4 Ways To Kick Start Your New Year

- Become accountable to someone in the areas in which you are looking for change and newness.

   The sharing of your faith becomes effective by the acknowledgment of every good thing, which is in you in Christ Jesus.
   Philemon 1:6

4. Expect The Holy Spirit To Bring Forth New Beginnings.
   We should have a great expectation in our hearts that new things and new seasons are going to break forth in our lives because this is God s desire towards us. It s just a matter of us agreeing with God s will and purpose for our lives.

   He who has begun a good work in you will complete it until the day of Jesus Christ;
   Philippians 1:6

devo 13

Keys to Life

10 Reasons NOT to Read Your Bible This Year

1. It Might Change Your Character

You may be inspired to treat people differently, to act on behalf of those who are mistreated, downtrodden, or hated. You may act differently not because you are trying to be a better person, but because you encounter a God who loves you just the way you are.

2. It May Change Your Actions

You may begin to think differently, and therefore act differently. People around you may see a difference in you as you begin to act in ways that are contrary to what the world holds as important.

3. You Might Think Differently about God

Currently, you may assume God is angry and disappointed in you, perhaps like someone in your own life. If you engage with

Keys to Life
10 Reasons NOT to Read Your Bible This Year

the Scriptures, you may notice that this isn't true about Him at all.

4. You Might Discover That You've Mistaken Religion for Relationship

You may realize the bad religion that you've experienced in the past is in fact very different from the Jesus in the Scriptures. You may actually encounter the Jesus in the Scriptures.

5. You May Give up Trying to Be Perfect in This Life

As you see the redemption in store in the Bible for countless misfits and heathens, idol worshipers and killers, you may learn of the restoration in store for your life too. You may be surprised by all the jacked up people in the Bible who were used by God.

6. It May Affect Your Relationships

You may begin to see people not for how they can benefit you, but instead how you can impact them. As you begin to apply what you learn in the Scriptures, you may see your relationships with others go to a whole new level of influence.

7. You May Become Unsettled

As you read stories of boldness and sacrifice through the lives of imperfect people, you may lose yourself in the stories. You may find yourself in the middle of a conversation from long ago. You may become unsettled with the life you currently live.

8. You May Realize That People Are Still the Same

Even though the world today is very different than in biblical times, you may find that people are very much the same as they've always been. You encounter people who are selfish, broken, and confused, but who end up being selfless, healed, and filled with purpose in life.

Keys to Life
10 Reasons NOT to Read Your Bible This Year

9. You May Want to Involve Others

The Bible was written over thousands of years by dozens of different authors, all, I believe, inspired by God. Its unique formation can make it pretty intimidating to understand at times. As you engage with the Scriptures, you may be compelled to bring in friends, family, or others to join you in your new quest.

10. It May Challenge You to Leave Behind a Legacy with Your Short Time on Earth

You may be compelled to give your life to a greater cause, one that extends far beyond your pleasures or comforts.

devo 14

Keys to the Marketplace
Part I

**Differences in the Roles of Kings and Priests
Part I**

What does it mean to be a King or a Priest? In Old Testament times a person had to be born of the Kingly family in order to become a King; they had to be born into the Priestly family line to become a Priest. But Jesus Christ came into the Earth to be both King and Priest. Now He sits at the right hand of the throne of God as King, and He is making intercession for us as High Priest. He rules over a Kingdom and He is building a Temple.

Here is some really good news. When you became a Christian you were born into God's family. You are now of the Kingly and Priestly family lines. Yes, you are a King and a Priest. Your primary calling may be to serve within the Temple (Church) as a Priest, or it may be to expand the Kingdom on Earth as a King. Either way, you will serve Him with your whole heart, and He will be with you, even to the ends of the Earth.

Keys to the Marketplace Part I
Differences in the Roles of Kings and Priests Part I

This understanding opens the door for marketplace ministry and the role of Kings and Priests to work together endeavoring to expand the Kingdom.

Priests (pastors, teachers, and other anointed church leaders) have a role in the Church.

Kings (Christians in the marketplace) have a role outside the church in the world, expanding the Kingdom of God.

Our attempts to close the clergy/laity gap fall short because God isn't trying to make Priests out of everyone or to keep the entire congregation busy (and introverted) inside the local church. Most of us have ministries outside our church—expanding the Kingdom. We are the Abrahams and Isaacs (businessmen), Joshuas and Calebs (military), Josephs and Davids (government officials), and Nathans and Daniels (Priests in government) of this present age. We can expand the Kingdom of God into every area of society.

The Apostle Paul asked the question, "How will they go unless they are sent?" (Romans 10:15). The implied answer is that they will not go. So I am writing to send you, to tell you that it is okay to expand the Kingdom of God into your corner of the world, to be a King!

Think about the great names that you know from the Bible. Perhaps Abraham, Isaac, Jacob, Joseph, Moses, Joshua, and David come to mind. Now, list all the Priests you can remember. Draw a blank? You may think of one or two Prophets, but leaders identified strictly as Priests do not stand out. Why is this? The reason is that God has always used Kings as the movers and shakers in the Kingdom.

Priests (pastors, teachers, and other church leaders) play an important role in the Temple (Church) in equipping the saints to do the ministry (in and outside the church). They keep families healthy by feeding them the Word. They counsel, encourage, heal, marry, and bury. They shepherd, feed, and equip God's people. Pastors naturally gravitate to a peaceful, healthy

Keys to the Marketplace Part I
Differences in the Roles of Kings and Priests Part I

atmosphere and have a Godly motivation to keep their congregations happy and maturing.

In contrast, Kings are aggressive. They establish their authority and they are willing to assert themselves. They move people into new territories—stretching people out of their comfort zones to expand the Kingdom of God on Earth.

Historically, Kings have been leaders who worked closely with Priests and Prophets. Kings were talented people with the resources to get things done where Priests were filled with the knowledge of the Lord. Kings were also well versed in God's Word and occasionally could operate in prophetic ministries themselves; Priests were understanding of the talent of the Kings and came along side them to encourage and release the Kings.

In the Old Testament we see that Daniel spent his life in a governmental, a Kingly role, but used his prophetic gift to interpret dreams. Abraham was a businessman who raised livestock and became the most powerful man in his day. Moses was a national leader. Joshua was a military leader. They all had a calling as Kings to possess the inheritance God gave His people.

In the New Testament, we see the Lord pressing major initiatives with Kings again. Neither Jesus nor any of the 12 disciples came from Priestly lines. The major players were Kings in the ministry sense. They had influence and power in the marketplace; some even had significant wealth. We see where there was failure to support the Priest (like the Apostle Paul) who many times were forced into outside labor (such as tent making).

Notice that the Kings did more than provide for the Temple of God and the Priest. This is important because some church leaders today want to release the Kings, but they think the King is to use all of his profit to provide for the Priests and the Temple. Of course, the Kings will be blessed financially, and they will be generous in providing for God's house, **but they are called to do more than that**. Kings have the calling of God to extend the

Keys to the Marketplace Part I
Differences in the Roles of Kings and Priests Part I

rulership of Jesus Christ into all of the world. They expand the Kingdom to fill the Earth with His glory. The separation between King and Priest is beginning to be exposed. The King is recognizing the Priest and the Priest is recognizing the King. Where the connection is made, there is provision and fruitfulness in both camps.

devo 15

Keys to the Marketplace
Part II

**Differences in the Roles of Kings and Priests
Part II**

In Part I, I talked about "Differences in the Roles of Kings and Priests." What it means to be a King or a Priest. In Old Testament times a person had to be born into the Kingly family in order to become a King. They had to be born into the Priestly family line to become a Priest. But Jesus Christ came into the Earth to be both King and Priest. Now He sits at the right hand of the throne of God as King, and He is making intercession for us as High Priest. He rules over a Kingdom and He is building a Temple. Today, **Priests** are pastors, teachers, and other anointed church leaders. They have a role in the Church. Modern day **Kings** are Christians in the marketplace. They have a role out in the world, expanding the Kingdom of God.

Keys to the Marketplace Part II
Differences in the Roles of Kings and Priests Part II

What is a Kings Priority?

Loving God seems to be a King's highest priority. The reason Priests have difficultly understanding just how much Kings love God is because they love God with a different mindset from Priests. You see, Kings love "serving lovers" not "loving servants" whereas Priests "love servants." You really can't serve those you don't love—whether it's God or people! People who force themselves to do what they really don't want to do, can never put their hearts into it and are seldom successful. Today so many Kings are forced into doing something church related that is just difficult for them because their hearts are just not in it. They do it out of guilt because they need to serve somewhere in the church to punch that guilt button (such as ... wave a flag in the parking lot or serve on the ushers team).

You see, to a King, serving means to build something. It means to be creative, be organizing, be leading, seeing things done with excellence. They despise poverty thinking and anything that has to do with a poverty mentality.

Both the King and the Priest love this scripture:

> One thing I have desired of the LORD, That will I seek: That I may dwell in the house of the LORD All the days of my life, To behold the beauty of the LORD, And to inquire in His temple.
> Psalm 27:4

They just go about it in a different way.

Why Love God?

David likely would reply that he was motivated by the pleasures of God.

Keys to the Marketplace Part II
Differences in the Roles of Kings and Priests Part II

> You will show me the path of life; In Your presence is fullness of joy; At Your right hand are pleasures forevermore.
> Psalm 16:11

Here's why Kings Love God – **It's so much fun, so rewarding, fulfilling, exciting.**

> How priceless is your unfailing love! Both high and low among men find refuge in the shadow of your wings. **They feast on the abundance** of your house; you give them **drink from your river of delights.** For with you is **the fountain of life**; in your light we see light.
> Psalm 36:7-9 (NIV) Emphasis added

Note: if I can't find the delight, the abundance, and the life...I'm probably relying on my own willpower to "serve" God. Your will power won't last a lifetime — you'll quit.

How do I fit?

God is not looking for robots to mindlessly carry out His plans. He's looking for those who will be bonded to Him in love.

> "In that day," declares the LORD, "you will call me 'my husband'; you will no longer call me 'my master.'"
> Hosea 2:16 (NIV)

Kings are God's partners and friends who share His vision for the Kingdom. "Serve" doesn't adequately convey what Kings do. They are Kingdom builders and **the Body of Christ needs to wake up to the value they bring to the Kingdom and the marketplace.** "Servant" doesn't convey how Kings view

Keys to the Marketplace Part II
Differences in the Roles of Kings and Priests Part II

themselves, or others for that matter. The Kings I have grown to know are some of the greatest servants, yet because of how they have been viewed in the church, they do not see themselves as such.

I say it's time we release the Kings to their fullest potential by recognizing their gifts and servant's heart.

devo 16

Keys to the Marketplace
Part III

Kings, Priests, and Prophets...Working Together

Nearly all of God's major initiatives in Scripture had the three ministries of Kings, Priests, and Prophets working together. When David was King, the Prophet Nathan blessed David's initiative to prepare for building the Temple. Nathan also pointed out David's sin with Bathsheba. Throughout Old Testament times Kings sought the advice of Prophets before engaging in warfare. Priests offered the sacrifices that went with those initiatives.

Certain functions were required to be kept separate. Kings were not allowed to perform Priestly functions. An impatient King Saul was sentenced to death for operating as a Priest when he offered sacrifices in place of Samuel, who was late in arriving (I Samuel 13:11). On the other hand, Saul previously practiced among the Prophets with no negative consequences (I Samuel 10:9-12).

Keys to the Marketplace Part III
Kings, Priests, and Prophets...Working Together

Highlighting some of the difficulties these three groups have working together may help to understand their differences.

View of Wealth — By a King's standard, Priests are typically far less focused on wealth and possessions. Pastors, especially TV ministers, who are overzealous for wealth seem out of place. On the other hand, some Priests spiritualize poverty and encourage others to adopt their simple lifestyles. They say, "Blessed are the poor," and they believe humility and meekness are clothed in "holy" poverty. However, Kings simply can't absorb this message. Their ministries in the marketplace are rooted in their influence and prosperity.

Without promoting the excesses of materialism, we must make room in our theology and churches for Kings to be channels for the finances, influence, power, and leadership to expand the Kingdom outside the church. If we release their ministry, they will bring evangelism to our communities and growth to our churches.

Leadership in Churches — The role of Prophets is to speak the voice of God. Priests have the responsibility to oversee and manage the local church. When the church undertakes large scale programs, projects, or fund raisers, they often attract Kingly ministries which can be tempted to run the whole church. Priests can never surrender the leadership of the church to a King without violating a spiritual principle. Kings don't serve God in the Temple; they serve Him in the marketplace. Local church pastors must never surrender their leadership to Kings who are called to function outside the church.

Decision Making — Our present theology places pastors of local churches as the highest authority and requires all activities to come under their "covering." A senior minister needs to be the highest authority in his/her church, and a Priest shouldn't be

Keys to the Marketplace Part III
Kings, Priests, and Prophets...Working Together

deterred from his/her vision for the church by Kings who are called to expand the Kingdom outside the church.

By the same token, when Kings function in the marketplace expanding the Kingdom, they are not simply an extension of the pastoral ministry in that city. Think about it. Historically, although Kings received guidance from Prophets and Priests, they made decisions on their own. Did David need anyone's permission to fight a battle? No. He heard from God and he took action. It was that simple.

Kings need to give themselves permission to hear God and act. They don't need their pastor's permission to operate outside the church. Of course, their actions should harmonize with the Priests', but Kings certainly won't get direction to function outside the church from most pastors. Kings are competitive, bold, creative, and decisive. For the most part, they will not learn to exercise those skills from a shepherding mentality.

Please hear this simple pattern for decision making. Pastors should make the decisions affecting the local church; they are God's Priests in the Temple. The tithe belongs to the Priest and Levites. Kings should focus their initiatives toward the great commission—reaching outside the church and expanding the Kingdom. Kings should return from the marketplace with fruit—fruit that grows the local church. Pastors function primarily in the church; Kings function primarily in the marketplace.

We do want to note that even though the ministry of Kings is focused on the marketplace, we still see them attending and supporting their local church; worshiping (and tithing) beside Prophets and Apostles.

City Transformation — We all want to see our cities won for Jesus, but at least here in the United States we have not seen it. Pastors have tried. We have unified, strategized, prayed, held citywide meetings, and tried to function as the gatekeepers of our

Keys to the Marketplace Part III
Kings, Priests, and Prophets...Working Together

cities. What has been missing, however, is Kings. Pastors have stepped outside the Temple and haven't seen the benefit of working with Kings in the capacity for which God created them. Without the decisiveness of Kings, progress at these pastors' meetings is painfully slow. Decisions require committee unity before anything can move forward. Whatever timely thing God might want to do (prophetically) is compromised in scope, schedule, and cost to make sure no one is offended and to be sure it fits within the church budget. The result— very little is done. No surprise when you think about it. The very concept of taking a city is a Kingly function that can be blessed by pastors/Priests, but not performed by them.

Apostolic Influence — Finally, it's worth noting that the Church is on the eve of a great apostolic awakening. Just as the Prophetic ministry came to the forefront in the 1980's, apostles similar to Paul, Peter, and James are beginning to appear with strengths in fathering, networking, church planting, and miraculous signs and wonders.

When these Priestly ministries begin to function, they will help release the Kingly anointing and bridge the functions between pastors, Prophets and Kings. There will be greater initiative and authority for bold new moves outside the church that expand the Kingdom— and grow the Church as a byproduct.

For future success we must understand the distinctions between Kings, Priests, and Prophets. All of God's major initiatives in the Bible were the result of these three ministries working together. When modern day Kings begin to function, we'll see new land taken for the Kingdom. Kings will begin to inherit the whole Earth as they possess what the Lord has for them. Pastors will see the impact of Kings in Church growth and evangelism. It's time to make room in our theology for this threefold cord.

Keys to the Marketplace Part III
Kings, Priests, and Prophets…Working Together

Learning to Equip Kings — Polishing a young King into that shiny diamond is a little like raising a strong willed child. They can be independent and self willed, and the finished product will function outside the church instead of inside it. They are best mentored by other Kings. Their best correction comes from the failure of their own flawed initiatives. We can help them most by pointing them in the direction of the Kingdom and helping them understand the value and place for their ministry. A pastor's biggest mistake can be putting Kings in charge of people ministries inside the church, thus introverting their focus. Kings can be pastoral to a degree, but generally with regard to the people in their own business.

devo 17

Keys to the Marketplace
Part IV

**The Business Leader's (Kings) Prayer Life
Asking W h a t s o e v e r !**

Christian business leaders (referred to as Kings) operate as friends of God and they pray out of the desires of their hearts.

1. The One Question God Asks Every King – The Solomon Question

It's important to realize that Kings may have vast resources, influence, and wealth, but they view those things as tools to obtain the desires of their hearts and of God's heart. Notice how God deals with Solomon's Kingly mentality:

> At Gibeon the LORD appeared to Solomon during the night in a dream, and God said, "**Ask for whatever you want me to give you.**"
> I Kings 3:5 (NIV) Emphasis added

Keys to the Marketplace Part IV
The Business Leader's (Kings) Prayer Life
Asking W h a t s o e v e r !

What's your answer to God's question?

2. He's Asking and Knocking

Instead of thinking of God's invitation to Solomon as unique, I want you to see it as a general invitation to Kings that can be found throughout the Bible.

> "If you remain in me and my words remain in you, **ask whatever you wish, and it will be given you**. This is to my Father's glory, that you bear much fruit, showing yourselves to be my disciples."
> John 15:7-8 (NIV) Emphasis added

> So Jesus answered and said to them, "Have faith in God. For assuredly, I say to you, whoever says to this mountain, 'Be removed and be cast into the sea,' and does not doubt in his heart, but believes that those things he says will be done, **he will have whatever he says**. Therefore I say to you, whatever things you ask when you pray, believe that you receive them, and you will have them."
> Mark 11:22-24 Emphasis added

> "Until now you have not asked for anything in my name. **Ask and you will receive**, and your joy will be complete."
> John 16:24 (NIV) Emphasis added

3. It's Important That We See this Theme in God's Word

> "**Ask and it will be given to you**; seek and you will find; knock and the door will be opened to

Keys to the Marketplace Part IV
The Business Leader's (Kings) Prayer Life
Asking W h a t s o e v e r !

you. For everyone who asks receives; he who seeks finds; and to him who knocks, the door will be opened."
Matthew 7:7-8 (NIV) Emphasis added

"Again, I tell you that if two of you on earth agree about anything you ask for, **it will be done for you by my Father in heaven**. For where two or three come together in my name, there am I with them."
Matthew 18:19-20 (NIV) Emphasis added

"'If you can?'" said Jesus. "**Everything is possible for him who believes**."
Mark 9:23 (NIV) Emphasis added

"Therefore I tell you, whatever you ask for in prayer, believe that you have received it, and **it will be yours**. And when you stand praying, if you hold anything against anyone, forgive him, so that your Father in heaven may forgive you your sins."
Mark 11:24-25 (NIV) Emphasis added

"I tell you the truth, anyone who has faith in me will do what I have been doing. **He will do even greater things than these**, because I am going to the Father. And I will do whatever you ask in my name, so that the Son may bring glory to the Father. **You may ask me for anything in my name, and I will do it**."
John 14:12-14 (NIV) Emphasis added

Keys to the Marketplace Part IV
The Business Leader's (Kings) Prayer Life
Asking W h a t s o e v e r !

"If you abide in Me, and My words abide in you, **you will ask what you desire,** and it shall be done for you. By this My Father is glorified, that you bear much fruit; so you will be My disciples."
John 15:7-8 Emphasis added

Dear friends, if our hearts do not condemn us, we have confidence before God and **receive from him anything we ask**, because we obey his commands and do what pleases him.
I John 3:21-22 (NIV) Emphasis added

This is the confidence we have in approaching God: that if we ask anything according to his will, **he hears us.** And if we know that he hears us—**whatever we ask**—we know that we have what we asked of him.
I John 5:14-15 (NIV) Emphasis added

> What if it is true? **What if God really will answer your prayers?** What if **He really is your business partner?** What does this mean for your business, your home, your family?

"... I tell you the truth, **my Father will give you whatever you ask in my name.** Until now you have not asked for anything in my name. **Ask and you will receive, and your joy will be complete.**"
John 16:23-24 (NIV) Emphasis added

You really won't know the "fullness of joy" available to you until you experience answered prayer! I challenge every King to

Keys to the Marketplace Part IV
The Business Leader's (Kings) Prayer Life
Asking Whatsoever!

ask, seek and knock (Matthew 7:7-8) . God will bless you and will use you to be a blessing to many.

devo 18

Keys to the Marketplace
Part V

Breaking the Lies of a Poverty Mentality

LIE 1. The Resource Pie Is a Fixed Quantity
The word of God says in Genesis 8:22 "As long as the earth endures, seedtime and harvest...will never cease" **TRUTH** — We are not going to run out of something we truly need. There are more than enough resources for everyone. That the resource pie is a fixed quantity is a lie will which become a scarcity mentality if you believe it long enough. Kings hate scarcity thinking!

LIE 2. It Is Spiritual to Be Poor
The cousin of "the resource pie is fixed," is another form of the poverty mentality which believes that poverty is an esteemed spiritual quality. Related to this, Christians often believe abundance to be excessive materialism. Mother Theresa had her

Keys to the Marketplace Part V
Breaking the Lies of a Poverty Mentality

own plane, a staff of 4,000 and made multimillion dollar decisions, yet people preach about how poor she was. It is not spiritual to be poor, it is not a higher calling to be poor.

LIE 3. The Wealthy Are Arrogant

Kings don't get this at all…the reason they have wealth in the first place is usually because they have already tapped into a spiritual principle at a deeper level than some of their poor but pious critics! God promotes humility.

> God opposes the proud, but gives grace to the humble.
> James 4:6 (NIV)

> …humility comes before honor.
> Proverbs 15:33 (NIV)

> Before his downfall a man's heart is proud, but humility comes before honor.
> Proverbs 18:12 (NIV)

> Humility and the fear of the LORD bring wealth and honor and life.
> Proverbs 22:4 (NIV)

LIE 4. God Will Automatically Transfer Wealth in the Last Days

We're not here to announce to the world that their wealth is flowing out of their pockets and into ours. That kind of message does not make converts out of lost people who have wealth. It scares them! TRUTH understood and acted upon in these last days is what is going to transfer wealth. Wealth transfer is coming today because Kings are beginning to stand up and take their place!

Keys to the Marketplace Part V
Breaking the Lies of a Poverty Mentality

LIE 5. Businesspeople Are Not as Spiritual as Priests.
Abraham, David, Paul, Jesus were pretty spiritual— not in the priesthood and not in full-time ministry but mighty Kings in today's world. Kings are waking up to the revelation that they are spiritual, have spiritual authority and God has a call upon their lives as much as any Priest. It's just different and therefore Kings must battle the lie that they are not spiritual!

LIE 6. Priests Have the Vision, While Kings Have the Provision
This stronghold presumes that marketplace ministries have no more use than to bring finances into the Church to expand its ministries under the direction of the pastor (a Priest). This is where the Priests inflict wounds in Kings. Many have felt rejection from Priestly ministry (by God or their pastor) and "used" when they are valued only for their offerings or some menial task.

When Kings Break Poverty Mentality, ministry will be accelerated in both the church and the marketplace! **I challenge Kings** to actively break the poverty thinking over people and the church. Step up to the place you have been called in these last days.

devo 19

Keys to the Marketplace
Part VI

The Kingdom's Effect in Our Lives
Part I

When we are born again we are translated into the kingdom of God. As a result, our lives are now being governed by a whole new set of realities. Kingdom realities now begin to shape us into the person God has ordained us to be. In the past our lives were shaped by Satan and his domain. Does your life reflect these new realities or are you still stuck in the past? As you begin to adhere to the new realities of the kingdom, your life will begin to change right before your eyes.

I want to talk about the kingdom of God and its effect upon our lives. More specifically, I want to talk about how our life and character values are shaped by the kingdom perspective we possess. If your perspective is wrong it will affect the way in which you carry yourself as a Christian and how you work out your salvation. If your perspective is right, it will enable you to come into all that Christ has desired for your life, thus enabling you to fulfill your destiny.

Keys to the Marketplace Part VI
The Kingdom's Effect in Our Lives Part I

The kingdom of God is God's rule and authority over any domain, sphere or influence. It is not only His rule over a future kingdom, but includes His rule in all of history as well as the present time.

Prior to salvation we were all under the power or tyranny of evil and sin. Satan ruled our lives. God has defeated the dark powers of Satan and has led us away to a new homeland— the Kingdom where His beloved Son rules. It is there where we experience the freedom of His redemption and of forgiveness of sin and removal of guilt. Salvation becomes a present experience of new living conditions.

People are shaped by the culture into which they are born. For example, when the early Americans first encountered the native Indians, they quickly realized they were different in many ways. Their values and lifestyle were totally different because of the culture they were born into.

- All of us were born into Satan's domain and culture. The Bible tells us that the whole world lie's in the lap of the devil. (1 John 5:19)
- The world is His domain – a kingdom of darkness.
- But we have now been translated out of that domain into the kingdom of God's Son.
- Therefore God now desires our lives to be shaped by His kingdom values.
- We should ask ourselves, "What kind of things have shaped my life and character? What has made me the person that I am?"
- What do we identify with the most? Is it our job, position in life, money, hobbies, interests, knowledge, activities, what we are good at, church life, musician, singer, deacon, elder, or whatever?
- What does your life revolve around? These are the things that shape your character and the person you are.

Keys to the Marketplace Part VI
The Kingdom's Effect in Our Lives Part I

- What is the center of your life or what is your life centered on. Are you being shaped by worldly culture, church culture or kingdom culture?
- It's important to understand that you were born into the kingdom and then added to the church. The kingdom culture comes first.

A Kingdom Centered Person is Rooted In Christ and His Kingdom.

> ...**rooted** and built up in Him and established in the faith, as you have been taught, abounding in it with thanksgiving. [8]Beware lest anyone cheat you through philosophy and empty deceit, according to the tradition of men, according to the basic principles of the world, and not according to Christ.
> Colossians 2:7-8 Emphasis added

> But seek first the kingdom of God and His righteousness, and all these things shall be added to you.
> Matthew 6:33

There Is No End to the Kingdom's Increase in Our Lives.

> For unto us a Child is born, Unto us a Son is given; and the government will be upon His shoulder. And His name will be called Wonderful, Counselor, Mighty God, Everlasting Father, Prince of Peace. **Of the increase of His government and peace There will be no end,** Upon the throne of David and over His kingdom, To order it and establish it with judgment and

Keys to the Marketplace Part VI
The Kingdom's Effect in Our Lives Part I

justice From that time forward, even forever. The zeal of the LORD of hosts will perform this.
Isaiah 9:6-7 Emphasis added

- Because we have been filled with the Holy Spirit, God is at work in our lives revealing new things to us all the time.
- The Holy Spirit continually searches out the heart of the Father and reveals His nature and character to us.
- As the revelation of God's kingdom continues to increase in our lives, the motivation to continually be transformed into His image is there as well.
- A person who is not kingdom minded soon gets stuck in a rut and continually deals with the same issues year after year seemingly with no victory.
- The scenery is the same year after year, which only produces a monotonous lifestyle that leads to complacency.
- There is an acceptance of the fact of being stuck in a sinful cycle.
- What is needed is a new perspective— a kingdom perspective that is ever increasing.
- It's like looking at a diamond and seeing a new facet with each angle; we begin to see God's kingdom in the same way.
- New facets or paradigms are always appearing, which continually gives us the motivation to move forward into new areas of character development. We're being changed from glory to glory.

If these kingdom realities are sown into our hearts we will produce the kind of fruit that God desires from each of us. We will be sincerely motivated to put on all of the characteristics of

Keys to the Marketplace Part VI
The Kingdom's Effect in Our Lives Part I

the new nature with a renewed vision to fulfill the destiny that God has charted for each of our lives.

devo 20

Keys to the Marketplace
Part VII

**The Kingdom's Effect in Our Lives
Part II**

The Kingdom of God Has the Power To Transform Our Lives.

> and what is the exceeding greatness of His power toward us who believe, according to the working of His mighty power.
> Ephesians 1:19

> For the kingdom of God is not in **word but in power.**
> 1 Corinthians 4:20 Emphasis added

There is a whole new level of freedom and deliverance that comes from each paradigm shift God takes us through. Not only

Keys to the Marketplace Part VII
The Kingdom's Effect in Our Lives Part II

do we receive the motivation to change, we also receive the power to change and be transformed into His image. Those who are touched by God's power are no longer slaves to sin.

> knowing this, that our old man was crucified with Him, that the body of sin might be done away with, that we should no longer be slaves of sin.
> Romans 6:6

> But if the Spirit of Him who **raised** Jesus from the dead dwells in you, He who **raised** Christ from the dead will also **give life** to your mortal bodies through His Spirit who dwells in you.
> Romans 8:11 Emphasis added

- We don't have to settle for the person we have become, because we now have the ability to change and be conformed to the image of Christ. As we grow and change, it has an effect upon the people around us as well.

- There is only so much deliverance and character transformation that we can receive from each paradigm we are in. We must continually be walking in new revelation of God's ever increasing kingdom to be changed from glory to glory.

Kingdom People are More Destiny Minded

Kingdom people become much more destiny minded than those who are not. They realize that everything they are involved in has an effect upon the kingdom of God because the eyes of their understanding are continually opened to all that God desires for them.

Keys to the Marketplace Part VII
The Kingdom's Effect in Our Lives Part II

> But as it is written: "Eye has not seen, nor ear heard, nor have entered into the heart of man the things which God has prepared for those who love Him." But God has revealed them to us through His Spirit. For the Spirit searches all things, yes, the deep things of God.
> 1 Corinthians 2:9-10

The kingdom minded person is concerned about the overall perspective of the kingdom and its influence upon the earth.

> And He put all things under His feet, and gave Him to be head over all things to the church, which is His body, the fullness of Him who fills all in all.
> Ephesians 1:22-23

You realize that you are a necessary part that must find its unique positioning in relationship to the whole. When your part is faithfully functioning in its place, whatever it may be, it affects the growth of the whole.

> from whom the whole body, joined and knit together by what every joint supplies, according to the effective working by which every part does its share, causes growth of the body for the edifying of itself in love.
> Ephesians 4:16

A person who is not kingdom minded often gets caught in the trap of simply functioning for the sake of ego, pride or self-gratification. When this happens we become a squeaky link or a grinding gear that detracts from the whole rather than adds to it

Keys to the Marketplace Part VII
The Kingdom's Effect in Our Lives Part II

We must have the same understanding that John the Baptist had— *"I must decrease and Jesus must increase."* (John 3:30) When we allow ego, pride and territorialism to interfere in our callings, there is a disruption in the kingdom that causes the flow of God's power to be cut off.

The Kingdom of God Encompasses Every Strata of Christianity That Exists Including All Denominations, Streams, Fellowships, Movements, Etc.

> There is one body and one Spirit, just as you were called in one hope of your calling; one Lord, one faith, one baptism; one God and Father of all, who is above all, and through all, and in you all.
> Ephesians 4:4-6

Kingdom Men and Women Operate with the Mind of Christ and the Divine Nature of God.

> For "who has known the mind of the Lord that he may instruct Him?" But we have the mind of Christ.
> 1 Corinthians 2:16

> by which have been given to us exceedingly great and precious promises, that through these you may be partakers of the divine nature, having escaped the corruption that is in the world through lust.
> 2 Peter 1:4

Keys to the Marketplace Part VII
The Kingdom's Effect in Our Lives Part II

The Kingdom of God Comes with a Rich Inheritance.

> the eyes of your understanding being enlightened; that you may know what is the hope of His calling, what are the riches of the glory of His inheritance in the saints,
> Ephesians 1:18

> as His divine power has given to us all things that pertain to life and godliness, through the knowledge of Him who called us by glory and virtue,
> 2 Peter 1:3

It Is a Kingdom Wherein Righteousness, Peace and Joy Dwell.

> for the kingdom of God is not eating and drinking, but righteousness and peace and joy in the Holy Spirit.
> Romans 14:17

If these kingdom realities are sown into our hearts we will produce the kind of fruit that God desires from each of us. We will be sincerely motivated to put on all of the characteristics of the new nature with a renewed vision to fulfill the destiny that God has charted for each of our lives.

devo 21

Keys to the Marketplace
Part VIII

The 1 Essential Habit of Every Effective Leader

The LORD said to Joshua, "Do not be afraid of them; I have given them into your hand. Not one of them will be able to withstand you."
Joshua 10:8 (NIV) Emphasis added

But as for you, be strong and do not give up, for your work will be rewarded.
2 Chronicles 15:7 (NIV)

I've always loved Joshua, who stood before his fellow countrymen at a crossroads in his nation's history and admonished them to "choose this day whom you will serve…" (Joshua 24:15) Joshua knew, as all great leaders know, that life is about intentional choices. And the failure to make a decision is, in fact, a choice in itself.

Keys to the Marketplace Part VIII
The 1 Essential Habit of Every Effective Leader

In its Latin root, the word *decide* literally means, *"to cut off."* In our culture, nobody wants to cut off anything. We are rife with procrastination; In fact, in some cases we reward it.

Many organizations have a decision deficiency syndrome. We have leaders who hesitate. They waffle and wait, hoping for a better opportunity. Let's be honest; you and I do this, as well. And it's killing our leadership.

If you want to be a better leader, resolve to be a better decision maker. It will revolutionize your organization, inspire your team, and liberate you from the constant worry of the possibility of a better opportunity coming along.

Here are three scenarios in which you should make a decision right now:

1. **You don't need more information.** You have everything you need to know to make the right decision. Sure, more information could make itself available if you wait, but if you're honest, you don't need it. You have the essentials, and nothing monumental would change that.
2. **More information won't come.** Sometimes, you're just stalling. In fact, most of the time, this is the case. We're afraid of consequences, criticism, or failure, so we hesitate. But really, this is just wasting time.
3. **Something will suffer if you wait.** More information might present itself, but the cost of waiting is greater than the cost of acting now and paying the consequences later. Your hesitation may be distracting you or keeping you from other work or simply frustrating your colleagues.

You can't do this with every decision, but you can probably do it with more than you realize. **Most indecisiveness comes from fear**. It's time to move beyond that and become the leader you were meant to be.

Something shifts in your paradigm when you resolve to be more decisive. You stop letting yourself be ruled by anxiety and apprehension. You become bolder and more confident. At first,

Keys to the Marketplace Part VIII
The 1 Essential Habit of Every Effective Leader

it may seem scary, but this is the key to being a leader worth following.

Sure, you will occasionally make the wrong choice, but you will never have to be afraid again. You will never catch yourself waiting for more information that isn't necessary to making a difference today.

It's time to decide. What have you been putting off?

devo 22

Keys to the Marketplace
Part IX

Skills Vs Gifts

His pleasure is not in the strength of the horse, nor His delight in the legs of a man; the LORD delights in those who fear Him, who put their hope in His unfailing love.
Psalm 147:10-11 (NIV)

Do you ever feel so skilled in what you do that you require little help from others? Perhaps you may feel that you are more skilled than any other in your field. Does God need your skills and abilities in order to accomplish His purposes on this earth? The answer is an emphatic NO!

One thing God does not need is our skills and abilities. However, He does give us the privilege of exercising our gifts and abilities for His service. That service may be as a computer technician, a secretary, an ironworker, or even a lawyer. God

Keys to the Marketplace Part IX
Skills Vs Gifts

calls each of us to our vocations to work unto Him. To believe that He needs our skills to accomplish His mission on earth would be to lower our understanding of an all encompassing and all powerful God. The psalmist tells us that His pleasure is not in our strength and ability, but His pleasure is in the attitude of the heart. It is what we find in the heart that helps determine whether ability is translated into availability. You see God is looking to and fro throughout the earth for a man or woman who is fully committed to Him. A man or woman who is committed to fearing the Lord and placing his hope in His unfailing love is the person God seeks to support.

> **"For the eyes of the LORD range throughout the earth to strengthen those whose hearts are fully committed to Him"**
> 2 Chronicles 16:9a (NIV) Emphasis added

When we allow His agenda to become our agenda, we can expect God to fully support all that we do.

If we want to see our skills and abilities multiplied a hundredfold, then we must make them completely available to His service. Where are the opportunities in which God is calling you to be available to Him? Next time someone asks you to be involved in some activity, before you say yea or nay, make sure you check in with the Master of our decisions to ensure that your gifts and talents are being used, as He desires.

devo 23

Keys to the Land
Part I

12 Keys to Understanding the Land of Israel
Part I

After being in Israel several times, I have been compelled to speak up concerning the land of Israel. God has much to say about His Covenant people and His Land. I have been broken (in a good way) for this land as God has truly changed my perspective and opened my eyes to so much concerning the land that I never knew. I don't consider myself an expert but feel the urgency to speak up about the value of Israel for our day.

The Land of Israel is the only place on earth, which God says He owns in terms of property ownership that can be transferred. (Of course, we know the whole world is His, yet this one parcel of land on the earth has a unique relationship to Him.) About Israel, He says,

Keys to the Land Part I
12 Keys to Understanding the Land of Israel Part I

> The land, moreover, shall not be sold permanently, for the land is Mine: for you are but aliens and sojourners with Me.
> Leviticus 25:23 (NASB)

We should never replace the land with a theology that eliminates its value and purpose in our day and for eternity.

Exactly What Does the Bible Say about God's Parcel of Land, and Who Has a Right to It?

When we come to the modern-day Israel-Palestine issue, people often ask the question, "Just what right do Israel and the Jewish people have to this land?" Arguments are continually brought forth concerning the rights of the Palestinians and the rights of the Israelis that seem logical to the people who present them. But a basic question still remains in my mind as I listen to the many conflicting viewpoints concerning this parcel of land; "Who has the ultimate authority to determine rights concerning this special piece of real estate?"

The biblical answer to that question is that God alone determines the "rights" that any of us have. Something is right or wrong because of Divine decree, not human feeling or human reason. The existence of God previous to the creation of the universe and mankind gives Him the right to determine our "rights."

Morality exists because God exists. Authority exists because God exists. And God has already determined the rights of Israel and the Jewish people to the land God owns and has deeded it over to them.

Let's look together at what He has to say about the Land of Israel, the people He chose to possess it, and why:

Keys to the Land Part I
12 Keys to Understanding the Land of Israel Part I

Key #1: The Land of Canaan, Renamed Israel by the Lord, Was Given by God to Abraham and His Descendants as an Everlasting Possession.

Notice God's own words said:

> The LORD appeared to Abram and said, "To your descendants I will give this land."
> Genesis 12:7a (NASB)

He repeated His promise when He said:

> "for all the land which you see, I will give it to you and to your descendants forever."
> Genesis 13:15 (NASB)

He later repeated the promise again:

> "To your descendants I have given this land."
> Genesis 15:18 (NASB)

Key #2: The Gift of this Land to Abraham and His Descendants Was Based on an Unconditional Covenant from God Himself.

> "And I will establish My covenant between Me and you and your descendants after you throughout their generations for an everlasting covenant, to be God to you and to your descendants after you. And I will give to you and to your descendants after you, the land of your sojourning, all the land of Canaan, for an everlasting possession; and I will be their God."
> Genesis 17:7-8 (NASB)

111

Keys to the Land Part I
12 Keys to Understanding the Land of Israel Part I

The sign of that covenant for Abraham and his descendants was circumcision. Twice in this passage, God mentions the everlasting nature of this covenant. There are some today who say that this covenant was conditional, that it was based on Israel's faithfulness to God. The Bible teaches otherwise.

This promise in Genesis 17 is still somewhat conditional, but in Genesis 22 God put Abraham to the test when He asked Abraham to give up Isaac his only son by promise. Here is what God said after the test was complete.

> Then the angel of the LORD called again to Abraham from heaven. This is what the LORD says: **Because you have obeyed me** and have not withheld even your son, your only son, **I swear by my own name** that I will certainly bless you. I will multiply your descendants beyond number, like the stars in the sky and the sand on the seashore. Your descendants will conquer the cities of their enemies. And through your descendants all the nations of the earth will be blessed **all because you have obeyed me.**
> Genesis 22:15-18 (NLT) Emphasis added

At this point the promise of the covenant us made unconditional. Further proof of this is given by God to Jacob when he is fleeing from Esau and has the dream of the ladder to heaven. In this dream God told Jacob:

> And behold, the LORD stood above it and said: "I am the LORD God of Abraham your father and the God of Isaac; **the land on which you lie I will give to you and your descendants.** Also your descendants shall be as the dust of the earth; you shall spread abroad to the west and the east, to the

Keys to the Land Part I
12 Keys to Understanding the Land of Israel Part I

> north and the south; and in you and in your seed all the families of the earth shall be blessed. Behold, I am with you and will keep you wherever you go, and will bring you back to this land; for I will not leave you until I have done what I have spoken to you."
> Genesis 28:13-15 Emphasis added

This is a confirmation of the unconditional covenant God swore by Himself alone (Genesis 22:16), which included the land later called Israel..

> This is what the LORD says, He who appoints the sun to shine by day, Who decrees the moon and stars to shine by night, Who stirs up the sea so that its waves roar -- the LORD Almighty is His Name; "Only if these ordinances vanish from My sight," declares the LORD, "will the descendants of Israel ever cease to be a nation before Me."
> Jeremiah 31:35-36 (NIV)

We agree that God promised to judge His people if they disobeyed Him. That is true for all of us. However, we do not agree with those who say that Israel's disobedience would forfeit their gift of the land and their national status as a people. Deuteronomy 28 shows that God's pronouncement of blessing and cursing only affected the quality of life of the Israelites, which was conditional upon their faithfulness. However, the promise of the land was not based upon Israel's performance, but upon God's oath and character – He will not lie.

Deuteronomy 30 shows that before they even entered the Promised Land, He knew they would violate His statutes and be evicted in a future day. Yet it also declares that He would bring them back into the land He had given their forefathers.

Keys to the Land Part I
12 Keys to Understanding the Land of Israel Part I

Key #3: The Land Was Given to Abraham and His Descendants as Part of God's Redemptive Blessing to the World.

> The Lord had said to Abram, "Leave your country, your people and your father's household and go to the land I will show you. I will make you into a great nation and I will bless you; I will make your name great, and you will be a blessing. I will bless those who bless you and whoever curses you I will curse; and all the peoples on earth will be blessed through you."
> Genesis 12:1-3 (NIV)

Israel was located in the center of the ancient world. All transportation and communication between the continents had to pass through this territory to reach the other. In doing so, the travelers, merchants and traders, and even the armies encountered the Children of Israel.

They were chosen for three purposes: to worship God in this land and show the world the blessing of serving the one true God of the Universe; to receive, record and transmit the Word of God (through them we have our Bible); and finally, to be the human channel for the Messiah from whom we have our salvation. In order for God to protect His purposes for the Children of Israel in the Land of Israel, He promised to bless those who blessed Abraham and his descendants and curse him who cursed them.

devo 24

Keys to the Land
Part II

12 Keys to Understanding the Land of Israel
Part II

After being in Israel several times, I have been compelled to speak up concerning the land of Israel. God has much to say about His Covenant people and His Land. I have been broken (in a good way) for this land as God has truly changed my perspective and opened my eyes to so much concerning the land that I never knew. I don't consider myself an expert but feel the urgency to speak up about the value of Israel for our day.

Exactly what does the Bible say about God's parcel of land, and who has a right to it?

The last devotional covered the first 3 Keys to Understanding the Land of Israel.

Key #4: This Land Was Not Given to the Descendants of Ishmael (One Ancestor of the Arab Peoples), but Rather to the Descendants of Isaac.

Keys to the Land Part II
12 Keys to Understanding the Land of Israel Part II

We should carry no bitterness toward the descendants of Ishmael, neither should we wish to be unkind to our Arab friends. However, we must be faithful to what the Bible teaches. Abraham himself considered Ishmael as a possible descendant to whom God would give the land.

> Abraham said to God, "Oh that Ishmael might live before You."
> Genesis 17:18 (NASB)

But God's answer was, and is, very clear. God answered Abraham:

> "No, but Sarah your wife shall bear you a son, and you shall call his name Isaac; and I will establish My covenant with him for an everlasting covenant for his descendants after him."
> Genesis 17:19 (NASB)

God promised to bless Ishmael and to make him a great nation:

> "And as for Ishmael, I have heard you: I will surely bless him; I will make him fruitful and will greatly increase his numbers. He will be the father of twelve rulers, and I will make him into a great nation"
> Genesis 17:20 (NIV)

However, the bloodline of the covenant promise concerning the Land would go through Isaac, not Ishmael:

> "...In Isaac your descendants shall be called"
> Hebrews 11:18 (NASB)

Keys to the Land Part II
12 Keys to Understanding the Land of Israel Part II

Key #5: This Land Was Not Given to the Other Sons of Abraham, but Only to Isaac

After Sarah died, Abraham had six more sons by Keturah, as well as others by his concubines. They are ancestors of many of the Arab peoples today, however, the covenant of the Land was not for them:

> Now Abraham gave all he had to Isaac; but to the sons of his concubines, Abraham gave gifts while he was still living and sent them away from his son Isaac eastward, to the land of the east.
> Genesis 25:5-6 (NASB

Note that Abraham even sent these sons away from the Land of Canaan.

Key #6: This Land and Covenant Were Given Only to Isaac's Son, Jacob, and His Descendants, Not Esau and His Descendants.

Jacob received the birthright from his father, Isaac when Isaac said to Jacob:

> "May He (God) also give you the blessing of Abraham, to you and to your descendants with you: that you may possess the land of your sojourning, which God gave to Abraham."
> In Genesis 28:4 (NASB)

But it wasn't simply the words of his father Isaac that guided the future of Jacob. It was a direct revelation from God Himself that convinced Jacob of his destiny. The Lord God revealed to Jacob His message about this land when He said:

Keys to the Land Part II
12 Keys to Understanding the Land of Israel Part II

> "I am the LORD, the God of your father Abraham and the God of Isaac; the land on which you lie, I will give it to you and to your descendants. Your descendants shall also be like the dust of the earth, and you shall spread out to the west and to the east and to the north and to the south; and in you and in your descendants shall all the families of the earth be blessed. And behold, I am with you, and will keep you wherever you go, and will bring you back to this land; for I will not leave you until I have done what I have promised you."
> Genesis 28:13-15 (NASB)

According to Genesis 36:6-8, Esau took his descendants and all his possessions and went to another land away from his brother Jacob. Esau lived in the hill country of Sear. The Bible tells us that Esau is Edom. It specifically tells us that the descendants of Esau are the Edomites, and Israel was not their land. The book of Obadiah is a proclamation of doom upon the sons of Esau (Edom) for their constant persecution of the descendants of Jacob (Israel):

> "Because of the violence against your brother Jacob, you will be covered with shame; you will be destroyed forever"
> Obadiah 1:10 (NIV)

devo 25

Keys to the Land
Part III

12 Keys to Understanding the Land of Israel Part III

After being in Israel several times, I have been compelled to speak up concerning the land of Israel. God has much to say about His Covenant people and His Land. I have been broken (in a good way) for this land as God has truly changed my perspective and opened my eyes to so much concerning the land that I never knew. I don't consider myself an expert but feel the urgency to speak up about the value of Israel for our day.

Exactly what does the Bible say about God's parcel of land, and who has a right to it?

The last two devotionals covered the first 6 Keys to Understanding the Land of Israel.

Keys to the Land Part III
12 Keys to Understanding the Land of Israel Part III

Key #7: God Told Israel to Conquer the Land Which He Had Given to Them.

> "See, I have placed the land before you; go in and possess the land which the LORD swore to give to your fathers, to Abraham, to Isaac, and to Jacob, to them and their descendants after them."
> Deuteronomy 1:8 (NASB)

On the east side of the Jordan River as the Israelites were about to enter into the Promised land, the Lord said to Joshua:

> "Moses My servant is dead. Now then, you and all these people, get ready to cross the Jordan river into the land I am about to give to them -- to the Israelites. I will give you every place where you set your foot, as I promised Moses. Your territory will extend from the desert and from Lebanon to the great river, the Euphrates - all the Hittite country -- and to the Great Sea on the west. Be strong and courageous, because you will lead these people to inherit the land I swore to their forefathers to give them"
> Joshua 1:2-4,6 (NIV)

Joshua then instructed his people with these words:

> "This is how you will know that the living God is among you, and that He will certainly drive out before you the Canaanites, Hittites, Hivites, Perizzites, Girgashites, Amorites and Jebusites"
> Joshua 3:10 (NIV)

Keys to the Land Part III
12 Keys to Understanding the Land of Israel Part III

He then told them how the Lord would part the flood waters of the Jordan River so they could cross over to the other side. This is what happened, and then the people knew that God was with them, and they conquered the land, region by region, starting with Jericho.

The reality of conflict over the land of Israel is nothing new and in no way indicates that God is not with the Jewish people concerning the land issue today. I have heard Christians say that Israel today could not be part of God's plan because there is so much war and strife that it can't be of God. However, since when has it been any different? All through the Old Testament, nations rose up to fight against the Jewish people, the descendants of Abraham, in the Land of Israel. From the moment Joshua brought the Children of Israel into the Promised Land, it was a fight to possess the Land. **King David was seemingly at constant war with his neighbors, the Philistines. Why should it be surprising that conflict is still happening today? The enemies of God have always fought against His plans.**

The prophet **Zechariah makes it clear** that at the end of days, God Himself will make Jerusalem a stumbling block for the nations and will judge them by whether or not they understand and support God's plans for Jerusalem and Israel. If they do, they will be blessed; if they don't, they will be destroyed:

> "I am going to make Jerusalem a cup that sends all the surrounding peoples reeling. Judah will be besieged as well as Jerusalem. On that day, when all the nations of the earth are gathered against her, I will make Jerusalem an immovable rock for all the nations. All who try to move it will injure themselves. On that day, I will set out to destroy all the nations that attack Jerusalem"
> Zechariah 12:2-3,9 (NIV)

Keys to the Land Part III
12 Keys to Understanding the Land of Israel Part III

Key #8: Israel's Sin and Subsequent Exile from the Land Did Not Change Their Divine Right to the Land Given to Them by the Lord in Covenant.

Many people have said that God's promise to give Israel this land was based upon Israel's faithfulness to God's laws, and that when they were disobedient and sent into captivity, this nullified God's promise. The Bible teaches otherwise. In Leviticus 26:40-43, we read that God would punish Israel for disobedience and send them into captivity. But, according to verses 44-45, God will bring them back:

> "Yet in spite of this, when they are in the land of their enemies, I will not reject them, nor will I so abhor them as to destroy them, breaking My covenant with them; for I am the LORD their God. But I will remember for them the covenant with their ancestors, whom I brought out of the land of Egypt in the sight of the nations, that I might be their God. I am the LORD."
> Leviticus 26:44-45 (NIV)

In Deuteronomy God promises:

> "Then the LORD your God will restore you from captivity, and have compassion on you, and will gather you again from all the peoples where the LORD your God has scattered you. If your outcasts are at the ends of the earth, from there the LORD your God will gather you, and from there He will bring you back. The LORD; your God will bring you into the land which your fathers possessed, and you shall possess it; and He will prosper you and multiply you more than your fathers."
> Deuteronomy 30:3-5 (NASB)

Keys to the Land Part III
12 Keys to Understanding the Land of Israel Part III

In the book of Amos God declares these words:

> "'Also I will restore the captivity of My people Israel, and they will rebuild the ruined cities and live in them. They will also plant vineyards and drink their wine, and make gardens and eat their fruit. I will also plant them on their land, and they will not again be rooted out from their land which I have given them,' says the LORD your God."
> Amos 9:14-15 (NASB)

Some opponents to Israel's right to the land say that these verses were fulfilled when the Jewish people returned from the Babylonian captivity. However, we know that there were other exiles and in-gatherings, as well. Yet, Amos speaks of a return to their ancient homeland, Israel, once and for all, when he says,

> "and they will not again be rooted out from their land which I have given them," says the LORD your God.
> Amos 9:15 (NASB)

That has never happened in history and many believe that the current return of the Jews to Israel is the final return that will culminate in the coming of Messiah.

Key #9: The Name of this Land Is Not Palestine, but Israel.

Twenty five hundred years ago, the prophet Ezekiel spoke of the restoration of Israel to its land in the last days. Ezekiel spoke of dry bones coming to life. Never before in history has a nation been destroyed and scattered all over the world, and then been brought back to life. It is a miracle and a fulfillment of Bible prophecy.

Keys to the Land Part III
12 Keys to Understanding the Land of Israel Part III

> Then He said to me, "Son of man, these bones are the whole house of Israel; behold, they say, 'Our bones are dried up, and our hope has perished. We are completely cut off. Therefore prophesy, and say to them, 'thus says the Lord GOD, Behold, I will open your graves and cause you to come up out of your graves, My people; and I will bring you into the land of **ISRAEL**.'"
> Ezekiel 37:11-12 (NASB) Emphasis added

Notice that the name of that land is ISRAEL, the land that is so often called the "land of Canaan" in the Bible. God says that in the last days it will be called ISRAEL.

The name, **Palestine, was a regional name that was imposed on the area by the Roman Emperor, Hadrian, who suppressed the Second Jewish Revolt in AD 135.** He was so angry with the Jews that he wanted to humiliate them and emphasize that the Jewish nation had lost its right to a homeland under Roman rule. The name Palaestina was originally an adjective derived from Philistia, the archenemies of the Israelites 1000 years earlier. Hadrian also changed the name of Jerusalem to Aelia Capitolina after his own family name, Aelia. He also forbade Jews from entering the city, except on the 9th of the Hebrew month Av, to mourn its destruction. Since he was considered a god in the Roman Empire, this was his attempt to break God's covenant between the Jewish people and their land. This effectively declared his pagan authority over Jerusalem, which had been the place of the presence of the God of Israel. To this day, the name Palestine flies in the face of Israel and the entire issue can be boiled down to a religious (spiritual) battle over a land whose fate will be decided by the God of the Bible, **since it is His land** (Leviticus 25:23).

Yeshua (Jesus), in describing the signs of the end of the age, said:

Keys to the Land Part III
12 Keys to Understanding the Land of Israel Part III

> "Jerusalem will be trampled on by the Gentiles until the times of the Gentiles are fulfilled." Luke 21:24b (NIV)

From the time of Hadrian until 1967, Jerusalem was controlled by Gentiles. It is now back in the hands of the Jewish people, which is one sign that **Messiah is soon to come to Zion.**

Key #10: The Stranger (Those Outside the Covenant) Will Live among You and Be Treated with Respect.

> They (God's covenant people) will rebuild the ancient ruins and restore the places long devastated: they will renew the ruined cities that have been devastated for generations. Aliens will shepherd your flock; foreigners will work your fields and vineyards.
> Isaiah 61:4,5 (NIV)

> If you (Israel) really change your ways and your actions and deal with each other justly, if you do not oppress the alien, the fatherless or the widow, and do not shed innocent blood in this place and if you do not follow other gods to your own harm, then I will let you live in this place, in the land I gave to your forefathers for ever and ever.
> Jeremiah 7:5-7 (NIV)

The **"alien" or "foreigner"** in these verses would include the Palestinian Arabs and other non-Jewish people who live in the land. They would receive a blessing by living and working in the Land of Israel, not the Land of Palestine. On the one hand, Israel must treat them with respect. On the other hand, they have the

Keys to the Land Part III
12 Keys to Understanding the Land of Israel Part III

responsibility to live at peace, abiding by the laws of the Land, recognizing under whose sovereignty it belongs.

This is what Moses taught:

> The community (of Israel) is to have the same rules for you and for the alien living among you; this is a lasting ordinance for the generations to come. You and the alien shall be the same before the LORD; the same laws and regulations will apply to you and to the alien living among you.
> Numbers 15:15,16 (NIV)

When this relationship is broken, as has happened today, then crisis ensues. Scripture has much more to say about the Land in prophecy, including the fact that Israel will go through many more trials before Messiah comes to fully restore Israel as the head of all nations.

devo 26

Keys to the Land
Part IV

12 Keys to Understanding the Land of Israel
Part IV

After being in Israel several times, I have been compelled to speak up concerning the land of Israel. God has much to say about His Covenant people and His Land. I have been broken (in a good way) for this land as God has truly changed my perspective and opened my eyes to so much concerning the land that I never knew. I don't consider myself an expert but feel the urgency to speak up about the value of Israel for our day.

Exactly what does the Bible say about God's parcel of land, and who has a right to it?

The last three devotionals covered the first 10 Keys to Understanding the Land of Israel.

Key #11: The Return of the Jewish People at the End of Days Will Be Initiated by God, and Their Return Will Signal the Restoration of a Barren and Broken Land.

Keys to the Land Part IV
12 Keys to Understanding the Land of Israel Part IV

The prophet Isaiah spoke of God's plan to bring His people back to Israel, saying:

> He will raise a banner for the nations and gather the exiles of Israel, He will assemble the scattered people of Judah from the four quarters of the earth.
> Isaiah 11:12 (NIV)

When the Jews began to return from the nations of the world at the end of the 19th century, the land was barren and sparsely inhabited. In the 1860s, the author Mark Twain traveled in what was then a backward region of the Ottoman Turkish Empire, called Palestine and described the land thus, "Nowhere in all the waste around was there a foot of shade." He called the land a "blistering, naked, treeless land." Of Galilee, he said, "There is no dew, nor flowers, nor birds, nor trees. There is a plain and an unshaded lake, and beyond them some barren mountains." His summary of Palestine: "Of all the lands there are for dismal scenery, I think Palestine must be the prince. The hills are barren, they are dull of color, they are unpicturesque in shape. It is a hopeless, dreary, heartbroken land."

This description matches Ezekiel's prophecy of the *"barren mountains of Israel"* in Ezekiel 36:1-7. However, Ezekiel goes on to say:

> But you, O mountains of Israel, will produce branches and fruit for My people Israel, for they will soon come home. I am concerned for you and will look on you with favor; you will be plowed and sown, and I will multiply the number of people upon you, even the whole house of Israel. The towns will be inhabited and the ruins rebuilt. I will increase the number of men and animals

Keys to the Land Part IV
12 Keys to Understanding the Land of Israel Part IV

> upon you, and they will be fruitful and become numerous. I will settle people on you as in the past and will make you prosper more than before. Then, you will know that I am the LORD. I will cause people, My people Israel, to walk upon you. They will possess you, and you will be their inheritance; you will never again deprive them of their children
> Ezekiel 36: 8-12 (NIV)

Truly, the return of the Jews from over 100 nations of the world is a modern-day miracle. Large waves of immigrants began to return in the 1880s. Since those early days, the deserts have been reforested, the rocky fields made fertile, the swamps drained and planted, the ancient terraces rebuilt, and the ruined cities of old reestablished. Israel is now a nation of over seven million people, a food exporting nation that boasts high levels of literacy, health, education and welfare, high technology and agricultural development.

Key #12: The Nations Will Be Part of the Return of the People and the Restoration of the Land.

The prophet Isaiah said of Israel:

> Arise, shine, for your light has come, and the glory of the LORD rises upon you. Surely the islands look to me; in the lead are the ships of Tarshish, bringing your sons from afar, with their silver and gold, to the honor of the LORD your God. Foreigners will rebuild your walls, and their kings will serve you. Your gates will always stand open, they will never be shut, day or night, so that men may bring you the wealth of the nations. For

Keys to the Land Part IV
12 Keys to Understanding the Land of Israel Part IV

the nation or kingdom that will not serve you will perish; it will be utterly ruined"
Isaiah 60:1,9-12 (NIV)

In Romans 11:11-14, Paul teaches that Christians are grafted into the olive tree, which is the covenants, promises and hope of Israel. We do not hold up the tree, but it holds us up, so we should not boast against His people, Israel. In verse 28, Paul tells us that they are beloved for the sake of the patriarchs. Without the faithfulness of the Jewish people in Israel, we would not have our example, our Bible, our Yeshua or our salvation. Therefore, he concludes that

> through the mercy shown you they also may obtain mercy.
> Romans 11:31

Paul teaches that Christians have a debt to pay to the Jewish people, by blessing them in tangible ways when he clearly states:

> For if the Gentiles have shared in the Jews' spiritual blessings, they owe it to the Jews to share with them their material blessings.
> Romans 15:27 (NIV)

How much more direct can God be regarding our Christian relationship to Israel and the Jewish people?

What Does This Mean To Us?
The day of Israel's full restoration is near. Messiah's return will make it possible and all nations shall live in peace. Until He comes, we who believe the Bible to be God's Word and that every promise of God will come to pass, must stand and support Israel's right to its land. It is a Divine right. We are patient with

Keys to the Land Part IV
12 Keys to Understanding the Land of Israel Part IV

those who do not believe the Bible, nor accept Israel's right to the land. Yet, with love for all, we must strongly support Israel's right. **We cannot do otherwise** and have clear consciences. We cannot say, on the one hand, that we believe there is a God Who has revealed His perfect will in His Holy Scriptures, and on the other hand, deny Israel its right to the land God promised to her.

Our commitment to Israel was penned by the Psalmist so long ago:

> "You will arise and have compassion on Zion, for it is time to show favor to her; the appointed time has come."
> Psalm 102:13 (NIV)

This is that day.

Again the Psalmist exhorts us:

> **"Pray for the peace of Jerusalem; may they prosper who love you. May peace be within your walls, and prosperity within your palaces. For the sake of my brothers and my friends, I will now say, 'May peace be within you.' For the sake of the house of the LORD our God, I will seek your good"**
> Psalm 122:6-9 (NASB77) Emphasis added

To Contact Phil Stern:
email - philstern@linkmin.org
web: www.linkmin.org
phone: 636-734-7771